From Poverty *to* Riches in Christ Jesus

SHARYN M SANTOS

WESTBOW
PRESS®
A DIVISION OF THOMAS NELSON
& ZONDERVAN

WestBow Press books may be ordered through booksellers or by contacting:

WestBow Press
A Division of Thomas Nelson & Zondervan
1663 Liberty Drive
Bloomington, IN 47403
www.westbowpress.com
844-714-3454

ISBN: 978-1-6642-1591-7 (sc)
ISBN: 978-1-6642-1590-0 (hc)
ISBN: 978-1-6642-1592-4 (e)

Library of Congress Control Number: 2020924635

Print information available on the last page.

WestBow Press rev. date: 01/17/2022

CONTENTS

CHAPTER 1

HUMBLE BEGINNINGS

James 4:10

The property at 651 Strand Lane, a place I called home for nearly eighteen years, will be forever etched in my mind. It is with innocence, unawareness and much ignorance as I look back reminiscing about my humble beginnings. *Humble* had a profoundly different meaning for me as a young girl growing up in a government-subsidized neighborhood. My mom was divorced and sick and her sickness was a constant reality for her. She was trapped in all ways imaginable. I was a product of her reality. The state of being confused and being alone in every sense of the word became my own personal reality.

I have one fleeting memory of a man who was carrying me up the stairs while scolding me because I was crying; wanting to go to school with my sisters. I would recognize this man as my father. I would not see him again until many years later when I attended his funeral. I would meet up with his family whom I knew no better than I had known the man who was part of my existence.

Everyone has a story, his or her own way of seeing things; each involving different circumstances and at times; different interpretations.

Later in life, I would find myself praying to my Lord and Savior Jesus Christ asking, "How do I defend myself? How do I make things right? How do I know and discern the truth based on the facts from my perspective, and without believing a lie? How do I take responsibility for my faults, and how do I refrain from owning that which has been so wrong?

I am a human being with the same vital needs that are crucial to all children growing into adulthood; the basic needs that equip us for this world. How does one find themselves playing catch-up years later, only to come to the conclusion that it may not be possible to catch-up in a cold unkind, and at times cruel world?

I wanted to be trusted. I wanted to belong. I wanted the rejection I routinely experienced simply to cease. I wouldn't want to impose my crippling hurts onto anyone. Is this just one example from my story that although you may not know me personally could potentially help you on some level from those hurtful things that are a part of your own story that left you emotionally, mentally and physically crippled. My experience of the many voids in my life personally told me a different story, one based on my own perspective with the constant rejections and the negative behavior of many, if not nearly all who crossed my path.

Being ostracized was commonplace to me. Although I may not have comprehended it as a child, my loneliness would scream loud to me whether I liked it or not. In fact, it continued to plague me for most of my life. I am speaking not to encompass the whole of society, but to describe how things were in my own little world.

I would find myself taking responsibility for some of my loneliness, as I would make a personal choice not to be part of "secular" society. I came to the realization that it would have been a temporary acceptance. That path would have been even worse. How much worse could it have been. I mean, it is hard to imagine something worse than the world in which I lived in.

Being rejected by others, and experiencing their unkindness in countless ways kept me emotionally paralyzed. I can see now it was merely a matter of which hurts I would be forced to live out. Hard-core facts simply do not lie.

One etched in stone reality I would soon be forced to accept was how I would personally fit the definition of a person who was impoverished on every level. I would equally learn that there is a silver lining to being in poverty; when those living in the same neighborhood are in the same position as you are on some level. I would unfortunately learn to the fullest the different levels. It is sometimes said that knowledge is everything. For me knowledge proved to be absolutely devastating.

My growing-up years, and the experiences I had as a child that turned out to be distinctly marked by poverty would never change. This knowledge forever changed me in ways that were at best bad, and at worst horrid.

Constantly being ignored and ostracized was a huge part of my life at home and at school. I always found myself at rock bottom looking up only to find myself spiraling downward. How does such a thing happen. Is that even possible. The depths of despair they call it. Emotional detachment, psychological wounded, and mental unpreparedness became my reality as I would personally live out.

Having no voice or an ounce of self-esteem to build on and nothing to offer society would be a dead end. I had no aspirations, no dreams, no clear desires, simply no way out; a shell of a person! I was alive physically but was dead in every other way. My hopelessness resulted in emotional paralysis which apparently began the moment of my birth and would follow me into every stage of development. The consequences of how I had to grow up in poverty would follow me right into my adulthood.

However, equal to my despair as a child, I would learn about the love of Jesus, and I somehow believed. I had nothing else. I was a candidate for everything going wrong as I look back. I desperately craved love, and when I learned that a man named Jesus who was God loved me; I listened. I would grow up hearing about his amazing love for all mankind.

I didn't ask questions, I was eight. A kind, loving and gentle woman held my hand and prayed with me. I kept hearing about this Jesus who loved everyone unconditionally and that included me. This idea was foreign to me. Looking back over my life, no one had ever included me, not that I could tell. So why would this Jesus love me? No one ever really loved me. My mom loved me; that's what moms are supposed to do, but when I was a child growing up no one in my own little world had ever told me that they loved me. For some reason unbeknownst to me, something gave me hope about Jesus' love.

It still sends chills through my body when I think of how desperate I was, and how different my story would be, if I had known that I was loved by others. I'm sure that a cult would have loved me to get its hands on me. False religion would have loved me to get its hands on me. Gangs would have loved me to get their hands on me. The wrong person with evil intentions would have loved me to get their hands on me.

But no, God had a plan for my Sunday School Teachers to teach me about the love of Jesus. John 3:16 was the first verse that I ever learned describing Jesus' love for me. God would begin to show me the true meaning of love, and the world's definition of love would not be what I needed. They would continue to explain the meaning of Salvation to me and somehow, I believed. The seed was planted in my life when I was a young child. God would take it from there and bring me to where I am today.

I saw other young people who were from my perspective truly loved, and I desperately wanted to be loved like they were. I didn't want to be invisible anymore. I wasn't ready for physical touch but I wanted someone to really love me, someone to show me that I deserved love. I had nothing to give back, but I became aware of my need to be acknowledged and accepted. I needed the kindness that I would recognize others receiving. Was it possible for me?

I soon learned that if I wanted to be liked or accepted, I would have to work hard, not disappoint, not inconvenience, not annoy, not anger, not talk back, and be grateful. I would learn this well. This resulted in many years of obedient behavior arising from a fear of rejection that has plagued me to this very day.

Having no opinion and always putting others above myself became my way of life as a child. This seems to sound biblical, doesn't it? I would learn the hard way that anything done by the world's standard is wrong, when you compare it to Gods' standard. Right or wrong, this mindset gave me hope of being accepted, liked and included. It didn't work most times. I was left to accept that this was my lot in life.

Having no hope that things would ever get better, I became as invisible on the outside as I was on the inside. I see now that I did not know for a mere second who I was to a dangerous degree. I was ignorant, unaware of my surroundings, innocent, and insecure, a victim ready to be used and abused. A recipe for disaster!

I spent those years in inner hopelessness and silent sadness. I could and did smile, talk and laugh at times. Apparently, I was seeing the glass as half full. Looking back, I see clearly just how lost I was. I gave new meaning to the word *voided*.

As I grew to learn more about Jesus, I began reciting bible verses and singing hymns loud and proud at times. I wasn't happy as others around me were, however there was something that made me sing, made me smile, and made me feel joyful at times when I was at church. Years later I came to realize that this was perhaps the beginning of God showing me exactly what was important, and it sure wasn't what the world screamed loud and clear. This knowledge would have a profoundly different meaning for me that would play out nearly a life time later.

As I continued to grow, I only became more aware of my deficits and my voids. I didn't fit in anywhere. I was ignored and stared at. I was left out, made fun of, teased relentlessly, and bullied. Going to school would define "bittersweet" for me.

I was always afraid that my mom would die any day because of her bad health. She was well-known at the hospital. She was on my mind daily, and I felt helpless in the face of her difficulties. She would sit on the front stoop at night and smoke. I would cringe and bite my nails praying that she would just come in out of the dark. I never told her how it scared me that she would sit outside late at night in a neighborhood that was so frightening. Back then children didn't have much of a voice. I discovered I had less of a voice than anyone who ever crossed my path.

I remember clearly when I was in elementary school, I would pray that God would take me first instead of my mom. There were times upon coming home from school, I would open the door to find a person from church waiting to take me and my siblings to their homes because my mom was in the hospital. She would become more and more sick as I grew up.

My innermost fear was that I would come home one day to find my mom dead. She had lung disease, diabetes, and rheumatoid arthritis. She would develop more health issues as she aged. I learned from an early age the definition of fear based on the circumstances in my young life, although I didn't have a clue. As I look back, I see the fear of the unknown was a large part of my story and even worse, I would soon experience it on a level that I could never have imagined.

CHAPTER 2

MY REALITY

Hebrews 11:1

I was one of the very few Caucasian kids in my school. I had a teacher in third grade who didn't like me. I attributed her feelings to my appearance. I was unkempt, shall we say. Although she was in fact a strict teacher, she could be warm toward most students. She favored the entire class over me. I obeyed her to a fault whenever possible.

I had a mom who drilled into her kids the idea that if we ever got in trouble at school or church, we would be in double trouble at home. I was obedient from the first day of my school experience. I would have done anything to get this teacher's approval, however her dislike for me would never give me the opportunity to gain her favor.

One time I was intently working on a map assignment, taking pride in my work for which I later became known for. After realizing that my pencil lead was broken, I immediately got out my pencil sharpener. My teacher wasn't attentive toward me and I was much too intimidated to ask her anything, so I began to sharpen my pencil without asking. The shavings were falling onto the floor. Her dis-dain for me was so intense that she with sheer pleasure scolded me in front of the class as she glared at me. I can actually still see her facial expressions glaring at me when I relive her unkindness to me.

All the kids were looking at me. I just wanted to crawl under my chair. She made a rude remark about the condition of my apartment. My teacher could obviously see by my clothing that we were even more impoverished than many in my neighborhood. I would have done absolutely anything to gain her approval. I didn't realize how desperate I was until years later when I would revisit my past. It's interesting that those memories of long ago are so vivid in my mind.

My mom was sick all the time. Many years later I would learn just how sick she had been as a child, a pattern that continued all her life. The hardest thing for me to accept about my teacher's treatment towards me was the fact that my mom shared her health issues with my teacher and she seemed to care. In a perfect world, this knowledge would have made a difference in how my teacher treated me. I wonder what would have been my mom's reaction if I told her how my teacher ignored me, and how she treated me so poorly at times.

My mom would voice to me her regrets in how we had to grow up after I was already grown. If she would have been intentional in explaining things to me as a child; this could have given me permission to share with her my own feelings. Perhaps I would have told her how this teacher and others treated me.

I recall another time when the same teacher caught me chewing gum in class. Very silently I may add, however chewing gum no less. I learned that chewing gum helped to take my hunger away. I earned the gum by reciting bible verses at church. It was a huge treat for me. I never got extra treats like this at home. Once again, the teacher made it a public affair making me spit it out. Then she grabbed her paddle and gave me two swats in the hallway. I was indignant. Having learned that word later in life I believe it applies here. Apparently, she wasn't aware of the other kids chewing gum in class. They were never called out on it.

Yet another time I was accused of doing something wrong and all I recall is the teacher grabbing my hand and hitting me with her ruler. That really hurt. Corporal punishment was well tolerated fifty-plus years ago.

I would be forced to see over and over again just how much this teacher disliked me for no good reason. My confidence in this proved itself to be true as I would graduate to the next grade taught by a different teacher who treated me differently. This particular teacher and others seemed to like me. I was permitted to help out in the classroom at times and was complimented for my behavior.

I would quickly learn that some kids chose consequences over obedience. They were either taken out of the class to be paddled, or spent time in the corner practically every day. They never seemed to learn the definition of obedience. They would disrupt the class daily in one way or another. Fighting with other kids or making fun of them never seemed to cease.

They didn't make fun of me at this point in my life. This would be short lived. My desire to be a helper in the classroom was frowned upon. "Goody too-shoes" would be the label for those who chose obedience over consequences.

As the kids began to figure out things on their own, and becoming more aware of their surroundings, the bad behavior of some of them increased as well. They began to identify the weak links. That would be me!

The bullies would soon reveal themselves to their victims in many ways. They couldn't get any lunch money from me, so they resorted to teasing me. One day they told me that I had to marry this boy whom no one liked, and of course I believed them. The tears flowed. Pitiful, huh? These kids did this practically every day as I recall. Although these kids were from the same economic background, they always seemed to fare better. Their clothes matched. They had new shoes before their old shoes fell apart. I never understood why they chose to bully other kids.

As soon as the teacher would be busy doing something other than teaching the class, the bullies would whisper to me that I had to marry this gross kid. I cried every single day. My stomach was in knots daily. As I look back, I feel so ashamed. What was I missing in my life that I allowed their behavior to torture me, and what was I missing that prevented me from telling the teacher or my mom?

I do recall when my tears turned into sobbing, they would say, "It's okay, you don't have to marry him." This behavior would be repeated on some level daily. Some days it would begin the moment I sat down in my chair, and other days it would begin while we were outside on recess, or when I was attempting to eat my lunch. My lunches were fat bologna and white bread. Being harassed while attempting to eat a lunch that gagged me only made matters worse.

Well, as we all know, once they got the reaction out of me that they were hoping for, they joyfully used it against me. Some memories of long ago seemed to be locked away in my memory bank until I revisited them three decades later.

I was afraid to tell the teacher, and so this behavior never stopped. I looked forward to the next grade only to discover that most kids would follow me. The bad behavior of some encouraged others to join in. We were warned about tattling on others. Otherwise, the teachers could never get their work done. The saying that kids will be kids had a different meaning for me in those informative years. The bullies seemed to have full reign over those whom they bullied. The worst thing that could happen to them was corporal punishment. Unfortunately, that didn't detour some of the kids. I never teased, hurt or made fun of other kids. I assumed all kids were the same. I never told my teachers, which apparently labeled me a target. The flip side of never tattling has served me well, as it has caused me to be trusted by others. I must take a measure of comfort in that.

I never seemed to escape the bad behavior on recess. They took the liberty to take the kickball away from me at their leisure. They broke into line just because they could. They would lie to the teacher when others would tell on them. This constant bad behavior stopped those of us who were rule followers in our tracks. I never seemed to get break from the bullies. Those teachers who treated me poorly as the result of my appearance seemed to make me an easy target for the bullies. I wonder where I would have been psychologically if I never experienced kindness from a teacher at some point.

My unawareness of society's way of doing things became part of my life throughout my growing-up years, and would unfortunately follow me right into my young adulthood.

Martin Luther King Jr. was killed when I was in elementary school, and it somehow changed the dynamics of my school experience from that day forward. We were grabbed up by our arms and ordered to run home. I was clueless until I got home, and my mom explained it to me on some level. Rumors began to circulate, and all eyes seemed to be on the Caucasian kids after that experience, all 12 of us. I would be forced to learn that the color of a person's skin came to the forefront after Dr. Kings death.

Prior to his death, my classmates didn't seem to see color. I know my family didn't. We never spoke of the fact that we were the minority. The difference in the shades of our skin color was never brought up until the day Dr. King was shot. Situations that happen can change people quickly and it absolutely did for me on that day. There was now tension directed at me by some of the African Americans, at least from my perspective. Unfortunately, time would prove my perspective.

I still had a couple of friends who were as ignorant as I was. This ignorance served us well for a time. However, things would begin to change that would affect me in negative ways per the obvious. I never knew what to expect when I got to school each day based on my own perspective of things. My insecurities began to grow and for me fear began to set in. As I find myself reminiscing about my childhood, I can unequivocally say that my life changed abruptly after Martin Luther King was killed. Children begin to lose their innocence when they are pulled into the adult world unprepared.

We were all just "normal kids". Girls played together and the boys played together. We played with what we had; such as jump ropes, hopscotch and tossed around marbles. We walked around or just engaged in small talk. Looking back causes me to compare those days of long ago with more recent times. I see clearly that each generation has its own memorable events that can be either smiled upon or frowned upon depending on their own experiences, and their perspective. Adults can use life experiences to either help or hurt the innocent, and psychologically young children.

My personal fears of the unknown affected me greatly as I was growing up. Some outgrow those fears. For me, my fears continued to grow. Forming children's opinions when they aren't mature enough to make sense of things on their own, robs them from thinking for themselves, and many never grow beyond what was planted in their minds and in their hearts.

I can say with assurance that I was terribly scared every day of someone hurting me. I never told my mom about my fears or my feelings. She never let on that she was scared and we never moved away, so I must have thought that my fears weren't credible. I lived in the same apartment until I graduated from High School. I would come to see the facts that didn't allow us to move and it had nothing to do with being safe and sound. I was left to deal with my fears myself. Unbeknownst to me, that would be the pivotal moment I would become invisible. It would unfortunately prove itself to be a reality in my life.

I lived in fear of the unknown. I also lived in the shadow of the real fear that my mom would die because of her bad health. That was bad enough, now I am scared whether I am at home or at school. I had a fear of being homeless, a fear of not fitting in, and a fear that God didn't love me, based on my lot in life. The fear of being rejected by mankind would begin my insecurities and result in my low self-esteem being played out in countless ways. The treatment of others and my own self-worth would begin to play out in ways that seemed to define me.

My apartment building was visible from the school's parking lot. I would usually run as fast as I could to get home before someone hurt me. One day when I was going home it began to rain really hard. The wind was blowing so hard that it caused my umbrella to turn inside out. I held it tight as it was blowing upward with my outstretched arm. I was petrified. I kept waiting for someone to help me as they ran right past me. No one came to my rescue.

I was sure that I was going to float up with the umbrella. With no one coming to help me, I threw my umbrella into the wind. It flew across the parking lot, and I ran home without a clue what could possibly transpire next. My imagination followed my fears. The fact that no one ever came to my rescue when I was growing up somehow resulted in me being a candidate for those who chose bullying as a sport. I wasn't protected by anyone, and the bullies took advantage of those with whom no one cared about. A quiet little girl that gave new meaning to invisible as time marched on.

After a week of disappointments in school, I felt it was somewhat better in that I went to church on Sunday. My Sunday school teachers would invite me over for lunch once in a while. That was huge in my life. I mean to actually have pizza, soda and dessert all in one day was a super treat. I tasted chocolate cake for the first time. As a result of my kids being accustomed to getting wonderful foods on a regular basis, I'm sure they never appreciated things quite the same way as I did. We can easily take for granted the pleasures of life that we get accustomed to. It seems to take away its "wow factor". Over time we don't have quite the same appreciation as we did before we experienced something wonderful and new for the first time. For those who only had the "best" from their start never experienced both ends of the spectrum.

I can say with honestly that my experience of tasting chocolate cake for the first time is still vivid in my mind all these years later. Not having the opportunity to cook as a child created in me a passion to learn to cook when I became an adult. Cooking for my kids and others has always been a delight for me.

If you don't experience things for yourself whether good or bad, no one can experience those things for you. Your left alone to appreciate only that which you know. Perhaps that is the reason why those who can't relate to a person in need can be viewed as being heartless. They will never be able to relate unless they walk in someone else's shoes. Those born on the wrong side of the tracks who finally escape it one day are better equip to relate to those who weren't born with a silver spoon in their mouths.

I loved the environment of my teacher's homes as well. I longed to be able to relate to them, and would have exchanged shoes with them any day of the week. Their homes exuded a peace that I didn't have at my apartment. Their houses were really clean. In addition, I felt really safe there. This caused me much guilt. My mom was alone in the environment of our apartment and I was safe in a clean house that was peaceful, clean, no smoking, and no potential drama; with yummy foods that my mom couldn't afford. I came to realize I was born guilt-ridden.

My mom did what she could. She made rhubarb pie with a few strawberries in an attempt to make it sweet; she put pudding in ice-cream cones; she would make cinnamon bread, and peanut butter fudge. On occasion she made beef stew and chili. Our staples were beanie weenies, spaghetti with sauce, salmon patties, and HER favorite, liver and onions.

Breakfast was puffed wheat and rice cereals. On occasion we had pancakes, homemade syrup made with sugar and boiling water. (a ton of sugar) Our lunches were bologna sandwiches and grilled cheese sandwiches. She did her best as I am now able to put it in perspective. I reminisce about those days in tears that are now gone forever.

Although life was unbearable at times, I can see clearly that it would have been even worse without a shadow of a doubt had I not been invited to church on that sunny afternoon so long ago. It's hard to imagine at times when I revisit those days that God did have his hand of protection over my family in those informative years. I just didn't see it.

After we began to get involved in church, we would receive help once in a while. One fond memory takes me back to a couple of women dropping off a spread of food, something that was foreign to me. I recall a fruit salad with marshmallows, and cool whip. It was delicious. I would find myself making it for my own kids years later.

I would later learn that someone ask my mom what her children would like for Christmas. I received a doll. I loved that doll. It wasn't like the expensive dolls of today, but it was everything to me back then. It made me feel "special" for a fleeting time. I will use that word, although it would never represent me as a child growing up in poverty.

Although holidays of long ago didn't have the same meaning for me as it did for some in my neighborhood, getting a doll for Christmas was special to me. Getting one from a complete stranger would touch my heart years later. Celebrations weren't personal to me. Birthdays were just another day. Going to birthday parties weren't in the cards for me either. I would imagine what kids did at parties. Sleepovers never made any sense to me as a child. These kids had their own beds, so why did they need to sleep at someone else's house. I would see the bigger picture as I grew. This awareness only teased me more. This became a normal way of life for me that I never embraced. My unawareness about life would begin to reveal just how voided I was.

There was a time when I was taken to a huge warehouse that had a ton of shoes. Someone was putting snow boots on us. This had something to do with the government. I thought the kids in my class would see my new boots and get the idea that I get new things equal to them. I must have thought this would lead to my needed acceptance. That didn't happen. The kids in my class knew that I was a safe target. For they would suffer no consequences for teasing me or bullying me because I never told on them.

However, one memory of a boy in my 4th grade class did give me a valentine. I can still conjure up those feelings of lone ago. Honestly, I didn't know what to do with his kindness. He never said anything; he just smiled. I don't remember thanking him. I used to think that my quietness was from being shy. I unfortunately had to learn the facts of my life, and it has always pointed to just how ill-equipped I was to a fault. I would never experience this kindness from a classmate again.

I remember not being able to see the chalkboard and my teacher moved me closer to her. She would tell my mom, which prompted her to take me to an eye doctor. So off we go to an eye doctor provided by the government to those who were poor. When the eye doctor finished my eye exam, he would tell my mom that there is absolutely nothing wrong with my eyes. He would say in front of me that I was lying. My mom told the teacher that there is nothing wrong with my eyes. My teacher would sit me back in my original seat. I felt so embarrassed because this teacher seemed to like me and trust me. She complimented my behavior in front of the class at times, and would choose me to deliver a package to another teacher. I looked like a liar to her now. I was confused. I was too afraid to lie. I would never put my mom in a position that required her to take me to see an eye doctor that I didn't need. I still couldn't see the chalkboard. I would become accustomed to squinting when I needed to look at my teacher from afar. My eyesight seemed to be even worse at my apartment. I would wake up every morning with blurry eyes. I didn't understand. Years later, I would come to the realization that my bad eyesight was from my mom's cigarette smoke. She smoked one cigarette after another. If she wasn't smoking one, there would be one lying in the ashtray burning away. I would have loved to find that teacher and tell her.

Church gave me some outlets and potentially saved my sanity as I see it now. Unfortunately, it wasn't without its own heartaches. I had the opportunity to go to camp for a week in the summer and I was elated as any child would be.

I remember all too clearly that my enthusiasm quickly diminished when I got to camp to find myself once again empty and devoid of all the skills, emotions, and material things that were extremely necessary that other campers obviously had. The stares of innocent kids looking at you as if you are under a microscope will bring a devoid person to their knees. Having no explanation for why you don't fit into any category doesn't make things any easier for you. The worst part was the girls in my cabin had no clue what it was like being me.

I would have been spared so much if there had been one other person like me. The two of us would have been rejected, ignored, rarely chosen, and made to feel invisible, however we would have had each other. To be lonely with someone else is a far better position to be in than to be lonely all by yourself.

The girls in my cabin threw their lovely suitcases around with their clothes perfectly folded. They had money to buy things. They had bathing suites decorative towels, special toothbrushes and toiletries that were foreign to me.

As for me, I had no expectations. I wonder if not having any expectations can be a benefit in its own way. I felt special that I had been invited to go to camp not thinking what was ahead for me. And I would have had a much better time if everyone had been like me. But no, once again I had to be reminded just how voided I was. My clothes were rolled up in a bag. I didn't have a pillow, a blanket or sheets. I had no money. I had no fancy bath gel and no special toothbrush. I didn't even have a bathing suit. I didn't know how to swim. I didn't know how to ride a bike. I didn't have a best friend, or even a good friend with whom to share the excitement of a week at camp. I was quickly ostracized the moment the other campers sized me up.

I ended up having some fun for the simple reason that someone had paid for me to go to camp, something my mom was not able to do. Being aware that this kind of life was not going to be consistent for me; I just wanted to enjoy it.

Having the opportunity to go to camp each summer for four years would continue to be bittersweet, as I was consistently reminded in every possible way just how much I couldn't fit in. This knowledge somehow did not deter me from going. However, by the end of the week I would have my enthusiasm snuffed right out of me. It would begin the moment I walked into my cabin holding my garbage bag filled with wrinkled clothing, and none of the necessary supplies that my fellow campers had.

I would see many of the same campers over the next four summers. I still have the same question, why didn't someone offer me a proper suitcase when they were aware that I didn't have one each summer that I came to camp. Why didn't my counselors ever provide me with those necessary things that I didn't have?

I didn't fit into any category. I received warm responses at times for my help. However, it didn't gain me approval. So, I continued with the same consistency as they did. The campers were as consistent in not gravitating towards me as I was consistent in working hard to fit it; in my own invisible way. In all fairness, I never asked to be invited. Perhaps my lack of necessary social skills would be the reason for their behavior towards me. I personally don't think this is the case. However, it does seem to soften the blow as I reminisce of long ago.

I would find myself always following others at a distance in hopes of joining in. I went down to the swimming pool to look around for someone in the shallow end, but to no avail. Those who knew how to swim didn't walk around in the shallow end of the pool. I walked around the pool and watched other's swim.

I wasn't aware that the stares of my fellow campers were the result of what I was wearing, shorts and a T-shirt, as a result of not owning a bathing suit. I look back and my ongoing question is; why didn't someone notice my deficits and provide me with a needed bathing suit. I was the same camper each of the four years with the same voids. They were some of the same campers that stared at me all four years, and equally were many of the same counselors.

Where were those whom loved the Lord, served him mightily, and were seemingly growing in their Christian faith? Why did they not take notice? How do you not notice when your cabin of nine girls, eight of which have what they need and you are the one in the corner with no blanket, no sheets, no pillow, no toiletries, no matching clothes and no bathing suit.

How does one not come to someone's defense? And what does it say about me who would gladly go to the same camp each summer for four years and not ask for help? Why didn't I ask for prayer that I was so desperately in need of? It must have appeared that I was ok with it. Otherwise, why did I continually put myself through this.

Having voids to this degree that results in a person being so invisible in the world in which they live in makes no sense. Being ignored by those who have the means to help seems to be a form of abuse on a level all on its own. I have concluded that ignorance can be a legitimate excuse for how kids treat and view others who are different. I see how much ignorance plays a role in the lives of kids who were born on the opposite side of the tracks of the impoverished. They just don't know it. Their bells and whistles of every kind can keep them in a proverbial bubble.

Following in the shadows of a few campers led me to the bikes. I had no knowledge of riding a bike, but I got on never the less. I was nervous, however I felt like one of the campers, that is until we found ourselves riding up a hill. By the time I got to the top half riding, half walking, the other campers speedily rode down the hill as I just sat there on my bike.

I didn't want the embarrassment that would come once they discovered that I really didn't know how to ride a bike. As they say what goes up must come down. So down I went. All I remember is that I held on tight and for one fleeting moment, I truly thought that I was going to die as I realized that I had no control of the bike. I simply closed my eyes and actually waited to go over the side of the hill as I was going down. I ended up at the bottom safe and sound. No one was there, so no one knew of my near-death experience. I don't recall having any emotions about that experience. I didn't share it with anyone.

There was always a long line at the canteen, as campers were waiting to purchase candy, ice cream, chips and soda. I walked right through not desiring anything, as I had become accustomed to never having any money. I found myself hiding in the craft house doing art projects. I was the epitome of a spectator. I wanted to trade places with some of those campers so badly. I remember an older camper combing her younger sister's hair. I wasn't able to put my thoughts into words as I stared at them. Years later, I realized that I wanted to experience having my hair combed.

Although I wanted to emulate those who crossed my path for countless reasons, I never developed hard feelings towards those fellow campers for what they had. The sad thing is I never felt worthy of anything good. It wasn't in the cards for me, and I just accepted it.

When I look back and visualize my bike wobbling to the left and to the right on the side of the cliff, my emotions overwhelm me.

I realize that only God could have protected me from injury or death that day. I don't understand why I didn't ask for help or tell anyone. I never told anyone how I felt. I never communicated to anyone my legitimate hurts, or pain when I was a child. That would be the beginning of how my life would play out on many fronts. Having such low expectations as a result of nothing ever changing for the better, I would be forced to accept my lot in life. From my personal perspective based on facts, no one thought I was worthy of anything better.

It was hard watching Counselors treat other campers differently. They hugged, laughed, and would show concern for them on different levels. There were 100 plus kids each year attending this "Christian" camp; they certainly weren't all related. Ignorance can be an excuse many times. I don't think this was ignorance. I was extremely sensitive to the injustices that I was forced to see day in and day out over the course of my young life.

If I were given more freedom to learn about the world in which I lived in, I can imagine that I would have fared so much better. I was like a sponge taking in all that my teachers taught me in school about things that I had no clue. I knew that I didn't fit, and my desires seemed to be different than the kids in my class. If I were given the choice to go out for recess or stay in my room reading, I would have chosen to stay in and read. When the weather prevented us from going out for recess, I was never disappointed. I would choose a book and read until we were told that recess was over. That may explain my own library at my home when I grew up. I never grew tired of reading books to my kids. They loved it as all children do. I didn't have many children's books at my apartment when I was a child. I remember reading the same book over and over. I wanted to read books about kids and their families. I would read Christian tracks and verses that were given to me.

The more I grew, the more I became aware that new experiences that were afforded to others never included me. There was a family who lived near-by who made homemade popsicles in dixie cups and sold them. Many in my neighborhood would get them. No money, no popsicle for me. This family included a father in the apartment. They would all be selling popsicles together. This example and others like it always stopped me in my tracks without words, until I grew up and learned more about my surroundings. I longed to have a family that did things together.

Another experience that didn't include me was when an ice-cream truck would frequent our neighborhood each summer, allowing very select kids to buy ice cream. It was hard never having what others had in my neighborhood. It was understandable when I couldn't join in with those who lived on the other side of the tracks. However, for those who were on the same economical level as I was, and watching them have what wasn't afforded to me never seemed to be fair.

After seeing this ice-cream truck come summer after summer to our neighborhood where only a few could afford their ice-cream never got easier. I can't remember the name, but they sold soft-serve ice cream liken to what we know today as "Dairy Queen". There were many more neighborhoods in a ten-mile radius with families who could afford to buy ice cream from that truck. Why would they come to a poor housing community that most couldn't afford to buy? "Teasing" would be a familiar word in my limited vocabulary. I would come to not favor this word.

A food truck would visit regularly in our neighborhood as well. Most could afford this. "Most" didn't include me. Thinking about it now, I wondered if those kids who could buy the candy, but not afford the ice cream could relate to my personal feelings of not being able to purchase either. Some things just don't make sense. I was always left feeling numb. Why was I always left out?

I would complete my 6 years of elementary school taking along with me memories of bullies and a few mean teachers, coupled with the unknowns that I was forced to deal with day in and day out. More examples of what "tease" would mean to me would surface on a whole new level, as I tried against all hope to wrap my head around going off to Middle School.

CHAPTER 3

FEAR OF THE UNKNOWN

Isaiah 40:10

How in the world was I going fit in, learn and grow in this middle school if some of my vital needs were not met ASAP? I simply had no hope. And now I am required to merge right into a whole new environment without even having the basics. I never caught up emotionally in my elementary school. *How have I found myself in an environment that I have no business being thrown into? Are you kidding? How in the world am I going to endure these next three years?*

The middle school was in my neighborhood as well, but not behind my apartment building as my elementary school was. It was seven or so blocks away. My mom never allowed me to cross the street, and now I am having to walk through backyards and wooded areas early in the morning even in the bitter cold of winter. My clothes were not conducive for the changing weather. I wore what was available. Style never represented me. Much didn't represent me unless it had a negative connotation.

We had rats in our development and even more in the wooded areas. When my siblings and I would walk to and from school they would run across our path scaring us to death. I am astonished that we were never bitten. They weren't merely a little larger than a mouse as one might think; they were nearly the size of cats. It was a nightmare. I opened my front screen door one day, and a rat missed my foot by an inch. My heart seemed to be in my throat. I do remember that I screamed. I also remember no one came to my rescue.

There were those kids who were up to no good in our neighborhood. We would hear ear-piercing screams, only to discover that they enjoyed skinning stray cats. Of all the things I needed my mom to share with me, this would be the one she chose to share. It was horrific. Drama seemed to be on every corner. No wonder my mom put up road blocks to discourage me from having a life. I'm sure there were alternatives back then. Regardless, her apartment, her rules.

That would be the easy part of my middle school experience as I would soon discover. There were many buses in the parking lot which was confusing until I discovered that the "rich" kids who lived ten or so miles away were being bused to my neighborhood school.

Fear gripped me for obvious reasons. Kids being seen and not heard had a profound different meaning for me. I mean, can't I be informed about anything. I didn't expect to be brought into an adult' s world, but this is my world, and I never seemed to be prepared to be in it. *Now these kids are going to learn a different definition of poor!* I had already experienced rubbing elbows with some church kids who had been born on the other side of the tracks. Their behavior towards me was enough to secure my fate in these secular kids ever accepting me. I was never encouraged to express myself so I would walk up and down on the sidewalk talking with God. I never made much out of it. I would have to grow up in every area of my life including spiritually to see, that although God never talked with me in an audible voice, he would begin to make himself real in my life.

I found that middle school presented itself with the same ole experiences that I saw others experience at church and at camp, coupled with a few new experiences, along with unknown fears that once again became a reality for me, something I never had the ability to gear up for. The first thing I noticed was how social these kids were among themselves. How happy they seemed to be. They were extremely happy. Call it what it is. And yes, they had things, purses, watches, clothes, and jewelry; some of which I had never seen before. Their books were covered with shiny colorful paper, whereas mine were covered with grocery bags.

As time marched on, the rich kids turned up with new clothes, new shoes, more Jewelry, and money to buy what they needed and wanted. I just wanted money to buy lunch items that weren't available to those of us who got free lunch. I would soon discover that they went on vacations, went to a variety of restaurants, celebrated their birthdays that included parties of all sorts, friends over on the weekends, and many were involved in sports and music. Some kids from my neighborhood could relate on some small level. They were the lucky ones. "Lucky" didn't represent me.

There were those who stared at me, and there were those who didn't. Needless to say, most didn't gravitate toward me. After a measure of time went by, I could tell by their actions that they wondered where I lived. After all, they didn't know me from their own neighborhood and they never witnessed me getting on their school bus after school. I would bide my time after school until the buses left to avoid additional humiliation.

With one humiliation over, now I have to get home. As I walked forward, dashing this way and that, I discovered that most of the people from my neighborhood would be out at this time of day. Outside! I later discovered that most of our neighbors began to awake this time of day, as the result of staying up all night. I just kept my head down speedily walking in the hopes that no one would notice me. Yeah right!

The stares alone gave me the impression that some had malice on their minds. The walk seemed endless. I realized that I was going to be frightened regardless if people were around in plain view or not. If no one was out, I would just feel a different kind of fear, but it was fear never-the-less. The fear that at any moment someone would come out of the woodwork. I didn't have even a slight chance to get myself to safety. I was doomed!

Day after day and week after week, I never knew what to expect when walking to and from school. I realized years later that my ignorance on every level potentially helped me in that I didn't have the common sense to really ponder the real dangers that were out there waiting for me. The fear which engulfed me was superficial in the sense that it protected me from seeing the life-and-death scares that were oh so real. I absolutely had no way of comprehending this level of fear.

To look back over these many years later has left me with the ongoing question: What prevented me from ever telling my mom, from jumping into her arms and sobbing, from taking a deep breath and releasing it as I arrived home. Couldn't my mom see my heart pounding so hard at times that my blouse was moving? Why didn't my mom ask me the pertinent questions so as to rule out any inappropriate behavior by others? Life was so much different in mom's generation. The world seemed to be safer than the world today. I wouldn't know, for I wasn't afforded the chance to learn about my world. I learned what the word "fear" meant because I experienced it personally.

I'm sure those fears that encapsulate me as a child and followed me into adulthood caused me to be extra cautious with my kids subconsciously. I was blamed for being much too strict and smothering at times. I was different from most parents because of my faith. I protected my kids physically and emotionally to a fault if possible. I took my job as a parent very seriously. I would discover later in life that the extra energy I put into protecting my own children, was the result of me not feeling protected when I was a child.

My children never went to bed without having story's read to them, prayers, followed by hugs and kisses. They never came home from school to an empty house. There were treats in the oven, surprises on their pillows, and so much more. I was always available to help with homework when needed. I loved being a mom. This is not saying anything against my mom. She would have done these things for me on a regular basis if her health didn't dictate her life. I remember her candied apples she made on occasion. Memory of her making popcorn balls one time for the neighbors comes to mind.

Middle school was hard enough for me to come to terms with; couple that with unkindness by my gym teacher for no good reason. She didn't like me from the moment I walked into her class room. She appeared to be an older teacher as I remember. She made it quite clear to me that she didn't favor me over the other girls in the class. The other girls looked different then I did.

They dressed better than I did, and had much more to offer; which would be proven by their countless stories and experiences. This gym teacher would just ignore me. I always had to be last. She never chose me to be first even once. I was physically there, but equally invisible.

I accepted her coldness, but to physically hurt me just because she could, was cruel. I recall being in gym class, and my gym teacher came over and jumped on my back. I didn't see her approaching, because I was focused on my exercises. The rest of the class continued with their exercises staring at me. No one said anything. I was under one hundred pounds of weight, and she was very muscular. It hurt really bad but I was determined not to cry. She walked away chuckling. I never shared that incident with my mom.

This teacher held such a disdain for me that didn't make any more sense than how those elementary teachers treated me. I wondered if they were all related. I was a rule follower. I obeyed to an absolute fault. Just another example how the world judges a person by their outward appearance.

My lower back is damaged, as was told to me by a doctor later in life. Apparently, there is scar tissue in my lower back. I wonder if she is responsible. I'll never know the true reason for my teachers' unkindness toward me other than the obvious. Back then I didn't have the tools to confront them, to hold them accountable, or actually forgive them. I never held a grudge either as I look back and relive those experiences. Not holding a grudge wasn't a choice that I consciously made. I wasn't given choices. I had no opinion. I just accepted my life, regardless how it materialized. I only felt the pain of what others did to me.

Years later as I began to write my story, and reminiscing about those who treated me bad, I would be reminded of the importance to forgive. I never thought much about the details of my life. I stuffed much of my childhood pain as to not relive it all over again. I do forgive those teachers because God commands it of me. He chooses to forgive his children and commands that we emulate him. "Matthew 18:22"

Thinking of needed forgiveness takes me back to a day when my mom sent me down to our neighborhood Dentist to have a tooth procedure. My mom didn't allow me to cross the street and now she is having me walk a couple of miles down to the government dentist that was in our neighborhood. I simply obeyed.

I would make it down there with no drama other than my stomach being in knots as I walked in sheer fear. I loathe Dentist's for the same reason as most, but to be forced to walk to a government Dental Office in my neighborhood by myself made the experience even worse.

This particular Dentist apparently didn't love his job. He seemed to like his clients even less. He shot me with Novocaine as quickly as he abruptly pulled the needle out before administering all the Novocaine to the nerve of the tooth. So, I was rewarded with a numb face, and a life-long memory of what Novocaine taste like. I would be accustomed to this torture until nearly all of my 32 teeth were filled with silver poison. Now that I have had a different experience with Dentists, I can attest you get what you pay for.

I would have my procedure and start back home. Dreading my walk home instilled more fear in me. Once again, I am experiencing my all too familiar panic. Whenever I would see kids walking toward me, I would pray that they would keep on walking. Looking down as I hurried home, I could hear people walking towards me. I didn't know most people in my neighborhood, which alone brought on fear.

I was inappropriately spoken too by a group of girls. They stopped in front of me so I had to stop. They began questioning me about where I was going. I didn't answer; first my face was numb from the Novocaine, and second, I was much too frightened. They began to touch me, and all I remember is that they left abruptly. When I began to write down these experiences I had as a child, I came to the conclusion that God had caused those girls to disappear in the fashion in which they did. I have a hard time remembering details, but they poked me with a stick, and the next thing I remember is how fast my heart was pounding. It was all I could do to walk, never mind trying to run for my life. I recall getting home somehow, and once again as bizarre as it sounds, I didn't share with my mom.

My middle school experiences would cause me to sink deeper into what is defined today as depression. Daily situations in which I never defended myself, would set me up for toxic people seeking to use me and eventually emotionally abusing me. I got myself little jobs so that I wouldn't have to eat lunch with those kids. My siblings and I got free lunches. I couldn't bear the additional humiliation day in and day out in the cafeteria. Food obviously was not a priority for me.

I have come to be told that I was operating in pride. I was unaware of it then. I went without breakfast and lunch from seventh grade to twelfth grade most of the time. I learned something, that if you deny yourself food long enough, your stomach begins to shrink, and you don't feel as hungry. At what point is a person's reality not defined as pride. Those who have no clue how my life played out on a personal level who judge me from their own perspective, reveals a level of ignorance they would never acknowledge or own.

My walk home after school each day proved to present its own unknowns, none of which ever become easy for me. On one occasion I happened to be walking home with other kids who lived in my building, thank goodness! As we were walking someone decided to speak gutter language addressing it to me. Ignoring this person instilled anger in him. He lit a cigarette lighter while walking towards me attempting to burn my hair.

I actually just kept walking. I could feel the warmth of the fire. Then someone got between us and told me to keep walking. All I remember is how numb I felt. I wasn't scared as one might think. Perhaps that level of fear bypassed being scared and what came next was sheer numbness. I came to the conclusion years later that I was seriously unprepared for my surroundings, and because of my position in society and my ignorance, others old and young alike obviously thought so little of me that they could actually hurt me for no apparent reason. What was this kid missing that he could do something so hurtful to someone whom he didn't know? I wasn't even close to being a threat to him. These kids must have transferred their lack of self-worth onto me. I couldn't even speak about it. I never told my mom.

My mom was peaceful with the neighbors and seemed to be well respected by most. She was very strict in my point of view, as were some of the other moms in my neighborhood. It just manifested itself differently. Most kids had tons of freedom in our neighborhood. I would have been much too scared to roam around after my experiences walking to and from school each day.

I would stare at the ground more than I looked up in hopes of no one seeing me. I didn't want anyone to misinterpret my facial expressions. I never wanted to find myself in a confrontation. I heard enough stories of those who confronted others because they looked at them the wrong way. This didn't always go well. I remember a kid staring at me from a distance, and something told me to get home fast. I began to walk faster which caused him to chase me. I dashed behind the apartment buildings attempting to lose him.

I was so petrified that I ran into my street instead of looking first, and ran right into a car that had stopped. The woman scolded me for not paying attention to where I was going. She didn't see the boy chasing me, so she must have thought I didn't have any common sense. I ran into my apartment and dashed up the stairs. I was never greeted by my mom as a rule, so it was common for me to go upstairs when I got home each day.

My mom didn't seem to have my innate fears. I'm not sure why I allowed myself to live in fear to the extent in which I did. A different personality, I would surmise. My mom was fearless as I look back. She would pay attention to her surroundings in the neighborhood when she heard things that were of concern. Perhaps that is the reason she was so strict. When there were noises outside in the dark, she would open the door to check it out. Who does that? Someone shot holes in our kitchen window one night and she went to investigate. I seemed to always be in ears view of these challenging events. Perhaps if I had pleaded with her not to go searching for a clue she would have listened. I would never know; I was silent then.

She finally got a car, not a whole car, for it didn't have a back seat. It was broken more than it was working. She was under the hood more times than I care to remember. I would find her lying on the ground under the car attempting to fix a muffler that came loose. I would be so embarrassed when other kids saw her crawling out from under the car all covered with dirt. The sad truth is that my embarrassment took precedence over my mom's health. He ongoing failing health should have prevented her from working on a car to begin with.

Our housing development represented mostly moms and kids. Men would visit regularly but most didn't live there, so my mom wasn't offered any help. I always wondered what the other moms thought when my mom was lying under her car, or practically inside the hood of her car attempting to fix it. They knew of her bad health. It took me years to figure out how to open the hood of my car without much effort. I'm not apologizing here. Just stating a fact. This car belonged in the junk yard. All of these acts of heroism would come to a halt when her ongoing decline in health would steal her energy, her tenacity, and her enthusiasm for life. I just don't know how she coped.

The difference between me and my mom is that I could get mad and angry at times, not really understanding it to the degree that I would later on; whereas my mom didn't seem to care from my perspective. My sense of hopelessness resulted in random outbursts that had no rhyme or reason. Had my mom already experienced these emotions that never changed anything, and all that was left was excepting the inevitable?

I was convinced that I was in the wrong family. I was convinced that I wasn't chosen. I was convinced that I had to live out my mom's reality. Being deficient in the very basic and necessary emotional and psychological tools kept me paralyzed.

With hope quickly fading, I would dream of being this person and that person only to find myself disappointed again and again. I learned quickly that day-dreaming was not a successful treatment. This would result in me simply giving up. I had no energy, no drive, no encouragement, no outlets, and no one to talk with on a deeper level—nothing! I was merely surviving. Life wasn't worth just surviving. Surviving for what?

Life would move on for me with the same consistency's; never having a voice, no opinion, no guidance, no leadership in the home, no encouragement and saturated with a level of ignorance that couldn't be explained at times.

However, in reminiscing about my 6 years of elementary school, I realize that I did learn much. I loved to read and did well in my subjects. I was actually pushed up a grade in those informative years. As I reminisce, I see how different things are today compared to when I was in elementary school. No one cheered me on when I skipped a grade in elementary school.

The teacher apparently called my mom, and when I arrived home, my mom informed me that I was going to the next grade. She smiled with a little laugh, so that confused me. I began to cry, and she ask me why am I crying. I must have thought that I did something wrong. She would then explain to me why I was moving up to the next grade. In today's society, there would be award ceremonies, surprise parties, gifts of all sorts, and in rare cases the news media would be contacted.

I showed up to my new class the next day, and the teacher warmly told me to sit down. No introductions, no compliments, nothing. She would proceed teaching the class. The world has looked at the outside of a person since the beginning of time. One of the best parts of going to the next grade, was that I escaped those who bullied me. I would still get bullied, but it wasn't as consistent. Those bullies in the class before was ruthless as I look back. I wonder if I would have had the courage to tell the teacher on them, would they have stopped? It definitely would have made my elementary years more tolerable.

I awoke one day prior to school letting out for the summer and my mom announces that I would be going away for the summer to work. No communication, no preparing me that I would be going away for the summer. No heads up. She actually was getting rid of me in an effort to protect me from the boys in the neighborhood. I wasn't old enough to work yet, and too old for the summer camp I attended the last four years, so off I went to a new neighborhood. Wow! I had so much hope of earning money and having fun. There was an above ground pool, treats of sorts, a bed with pillows and actual sheets and air-conditioning. What more could I ask for?

This should have been the time of my life. I had a little bit of freedom. I made a dollar each week for cleaning. I had some yummy food choices, of which I didn't get to experience very often. However, I would quickly learn that I shouldn't judge a book by its cover. A tremendous amount of alcohol would be circulating with neighbors and friends on the weekends.

I never knew the whole picture of the lives of these people. I knew that they worked and that their family was very privileged compared to mine. The meaning of not judging a book by its cover was well taught to me this particular summer. They had so many material things and lots of money. They apparently had many friends. One memory of that summer was seeing how much they enjoyed showing off all that they had to whomever was watching. That would be me. They had shoes that matched their outfits. Money overflowing in glass piggybanks that landed on the floor; and was never picked up.

They seemed to enjoy an audience when playing their instruments. That would be me again. They swam like little fish. I watched them swim like fish. I was thrown into the water to learn how to swim. I didn't learn to swim because I was too focused on choking to death. They forgot to tell me to hold my breath as I was plunged to the bottom. I couldn't wrap my head around why they would do that to me while laughing, and I can't wrap my head around it to this day.

I remember buying matching tennis shoes for my outfits when I grew up. I never connected those dots, until I began to write my story years later. These particular people knew that my only pair of shoes had holes in them. They seemed to just turn a blind eye, at least from my perspective. Otherwise, it would have gained me new shoes, correct?

As the summer carried on, my introduction to alcohol, and how it changes people began to scare me. Words and actions were dramatically changed in those who drank compared to when they didn't. My chores increased with no additional money, so all in all my anticipation of a great summer quickly faded. I had already accepted that the disappointments in life was the norm for me. I must have thought geographics would change my personal "norm" this particular summer.

I proved my work ethics by all the extra things I did without being told. I kept the yard tidy, watered the flowers, cleaned the outdoor tables, cleaned the house, and kept the dishes from piling up, cleaned the basement for their parties, all of which were in addition to my normal chores. I felt as if it was my own little house that summer.

I took pride in keeping it tidy. I attempted to do the same at my apartment to no avail. I would find myself cleaning houses for nearly thirty years, and although it wasn't always enjoyable or easy at times, it served me well. It allowed me to be home to see my kids off to school, and to greet them each day after school.

I soon learned that so-called freedom is not so free and that strings attached are a big negative. The enthusiasm that I had when I first learned that I would be away for the summer and having the chance to make money was sheer delight. I didn't earn the amount of money that I deserved. I didn't understand until years later why I had such sick feelings in my stomach during that summer. The memory of that summer brings back those same feelings.

Once again, I never shared with my mom how hard I worked that summer. I always wanted to ask her if she knew how my summer would play out. Did she realize that she teased me in making me believe that it was a special treat for me to go away that summer? My mom would have benefited greatly from all the food that was wasted that summer. I didn't even make enough to help her either. We never starved but the choices were slim. Because of my distaste for milk, cereal, cheese, and white bread, my stomach would have a different opinion at times. One disappointment after another didn't give me much to hope for. I found myself working hard to not get my hopes up. I guess it was my way of guarding myself.

I would quickly learn that the disappointments of food would be the norm for me; equal to the many teases I endured. Unbeknownst to me at the time was what was in store for me, that would follow me along my life's journey. The teases would cause me to not trust people because the end result was always the same: disappointment. You unfortunately loop the potential sincere people in with those who seem to take pleasure in teasing you with things that are out of your reach. You find yourself not trusting anyone.

I knew what rejection was. I knew what unkindness was to the fullest degree. I was accustomed to being ostracized and I had too many voids to count, but to be taken advantage of and cheated out of a fair wage for the work I did that summer set me back emotionally, if such a thing were even possible. This experience somehow didn't prepare me for what was in store for me when I grew up. I was the epitome of clueless.

However, I did get to go shopping to buy clothes with the money that I worked so hard for. This was my first experience of actually going to the store and picking out something for myself. I remember every single detail as I reminisce of long ago. Going shopping was not the norm for me. I had my own definition of "norm" and it wouldn't be envied by anyone.

I didn't know for certain what I could buy with the amount of money that I had earned, but I was excited. This mom planned to take her girls shopping and they invited me to go along. I would find myself shopping alone. I didn't think anything about it. We would arrive at the cashier at the same time. They had two carts filled to the brim, and I had a cart that was not necessary for my items. I used the cart because it was part of the whole experience, or so I thought. My enthusiasm began to somewhat dimmish when I saw how full their two carts were.

Nevertheless, I had a warm cashier ringing up my purchases. When it was all done, I handed the cashier my money; she smiled and told me that I was short two dollars. I thought that I added my money up correctly, but I was short. I looked at the family behind me, and they just glared right back at me. I proceeded to put back an article of clothing that I didn't have enough money for. I was embarrassed to say the least. I noticed that the cashier wasn't as warm with them as she was with me. It is amazing how we can act towards one another and assume no one notices. The cashier noticed. However, with all that to say, I was thankful for my skirt and matching jacket that I worked for and purchased myself.

Summer would come to an end, and another year at middle school would begin. I never experienced the excitement and joy that my kids and their friends had in going off to school with new clothes, and new shoes. I never had either. My on-going disappointments was sown into the fabric of my very being. However, this first day of school would be different, it would be the first time in my school experience that I was able to wear something new on the first day. Unfortunately, it was short lived. I had to accept that my peers would always supersede anything I had. Nothing got me out of that neighborhood. My mom's health never changed for the better.

My disappointment with how the summer played out still superseded going back to my apartment. Everything superseded going back to my apartment. I would dream of someone rescuing me from that place. Needless to say, the first day of school came if I was emotionally ready or not. I would begin my first day back to school dashing behind apartments absolutely numb. I can still conjure up those feelings of knots in my stomach of long ago.

I had never experienced going school shopping with my mom as some in my neighborhood had. On the contrary my mom expected her children to help financially when they were old enough to work. That would be at the ripe old age of 13. Making money replaced learning about the world in which I was born into. It was a priority; out of necessity. It was all about surviving in a world that didn't seem to care if some were alive or dead.

CHAPTER 4

READY OR NOT

Psalm 32:8

Ready or not in any language, I would find myself embarking on a new chapter in my young life. I was 13 "chronologically".

My very first job was working side by side with preschool teachers in a summer program that was available to moms of young children who lived in the inner city. They didn't have preschools as they do today. These children were being prepared for kindergarten. This job led me to work with children on many levels throughout my life. I recall a little boy who warmed up to me fast, and wanted me to sit with him. He seemed sad and lonely. I helped him with his school papers, and sat with him as he ate his lunch.

There were approximately fifteen kids in our class. Over time this little boy began asking me to stay with him when it was time for him to go home. I assured him that I would be back in the morning. He slowly began sharing me about his mom, saying that she made him stand in the hallway of their apartment building when she got mad at him. I felt his heart, but I obviously didn't have the tools to go any farther. I didn't notice any marks on his arms, legs, or face. The possibility that he could be in real danger never crossed my mind.

When I helped serve the kids lunch, I could see how hungry this little boy was. I would think of him at night with tenderness. God gives each of us a heart for others. It's what one does with it that matters. What could I have done to make sure that this little boy and others like him were not abused or neglected? I realize that I was a young teenager without the experience needed to be in leadership, however, I should have had the knowledge to get help. Lack of knowledge prevents you from being a productive citizen. Reminiscing reminds me of how voided I was in every stage of development.

My next summer job would be working at a rehabilitation facility as a nurse's aide. This involved feeding patients who were paralyzed, transporting them to various classes and keeping them company.

There was this particular woman whose life had been spared after a vacation bus went off a cliff, paralyzing her from the neck down. Not easy to watch. She was young when the accident happened. She enjoyed my company, and we became friends. I would begin to feed her one day, not realizing that I was feeding her too fast and she began to choke. She smiled and shook her head indicating that I should slow down. I felt very stupid. Speaking of her now gives me a little sick feeling in my stomach.

I would learn that this quadriplegic woman's mom had gained a great deal of money by suing the bus company. She was the one who had put her daughter in this government-subsidized facility. When the paralyzed woman eventually shared this story with me, I could see the hurt in her eyes. She mentioned that her mom rarely visited her.

I would venture to say based on how I conducted myself at this facility, this woman thought I had it all together financially and otherwise. She never knew that her stories about her life before her accident and my life were polar opposite. I didn't have the heart to tell her how pitiful my life was up to this point. Her position in life as a result of her accident superseded any complaints I had, even with the hard-core facts of my life.

I became well known for helping out and socializing with the patients. It seemed to help the patients with the boredom that comes from depending on others day in and day out in a rehabilitation facility.

I recall an African American man whom I helped as well. His paralysis was the result of a head-on collision by a drunk driver when he was a very young man. We began to talk regularly. He had no idea that I equally came from the same side of the tracks as he did. I never let on. I never lied to anyone about my life; I just declined to share my life with anyone. I became ashamed and embarrassed by how I had to live. I operated in this manner for years.

This young man assumed that I had the life he dreamed about, based on how I conducted myself. I feared he would ask me questions that would expose who I was and where I had to live. He mistook my quietness for just being shy. My heart wouldn't allow me to share my hurts and concerns with a man who would die in a nursing home facility.

I would stay longer at the nursing home at times to postpone the ongoing fear of having to get on a metro bus. This was my first experience of riding a metro bus, and it never seemed to get any easier. No one ever knew of my ongoing fears.

One day the bus that I transferred from was late, or perhaps I somehow missed it. I waited longer than I was accustomed to and called my mom from a pay-ed phone. I told her that I was still sitting on a bench waiting for the bus. Even though my voice had trembled, she told me to just wait there until the next bus came by. It was beginning to get dark and began to rain. I was very scared.

After a short time went by, a truck sped by and slowed down. There were two boys in the back who tried to entice me to get on the truck. That incident just about sent me over the edge. I doubt that my mom would have smiled at the idea of me jumping in the back of any truck, let alone in a complete stranger's truck. If the bus had not shown up when it did, I think I would have died. How much can a frightened heart withstand?

I would finally get home saying nothing of the entire experience. If my mom would have rescued me when the bus was late, she could have spared me additional fears. I never really questioned my mom for not meeting my needs. By this stage of my development, it was just the way life was for me. Even though my life never changed for the better, I never chose to embrace it. My numbness and shutting down wasn't really accepting it; it was mere survival.

As this job ended for the summer, I would be offered a part-time job on the weekends, but my mom vetoed that. She was thinking of the winter approaching and didn't think it was a wise decision. I was disappointed because I knew the patients would miss me. We could have used the money as well. However, with that to say, I would come to realize years later that my mom's decision to not allow me to work as a result of the potential bad weather conveyed to me that she did in fact love me. I could have benefited greatly from a few words of encouragement along the way in those growing up years.

I may not have had the high self-esteem that most who crossed my path did, but I can say with certainty that God gave me a tenderness for others. The physical condition that these patients were in, was absolutely heart wrenching. The sad thing is although it would break my heart, it didn't cause me to feel better about my life. I would be forced to live in a society that seemed to never notice me, and their treatment and rejection at times was numbing.

My mom never poured into me what I needed, but she was in total control. There was a measure of security in that. She was the boss every step of the way even when her health declined to the point that she didn't seem to be in charge. I knew what she expected. The real fear of her dying was always in the back of my mind, so this kept me on the straight and narrow; more "straight" than I really wanted. So, I kept myself busy by working as much as I could. This kept me focused on making money to buy the necessities.

As I look back and reminisce about my mom, I liken it to a blank canvas, where nothing has yet been planned or decided. She never had the opportunity to move forward or grow to complete her blank canvas. I would catch glimpses of my mom shutting down and giving up against all odds; being forced to accept life for what it was. She simply gave up the fight because things never changed for the better in her life. The guilt of how my mom had to live didn't allow me to question, or blame her.

I see clearly that I truly was a product of my environment. I was forced to come to the realization that I too had no hope of anything ever changing for me. Life for me was simply existing.

My mom's health would go from really bad to hopeless. The only times she went out was to go to the doctor or the grocery store. She took so many pharmaceutical drugs that she smelled like the medicine she took. Her diabetes was rarely under control. Her body wouldn't react to certain drugs. She simply became a guinea pig for the doctors. Because my mom had to depend on the government for all her medicines, surgeries, and doctor's visits, needless to say she wasn't treated like those who paid their way.

Her poor body just could not take it anymore. She would die at fifty-one years of age, leaving behind a six-year-old grandson who truly loved her and she equally adored him, and a granddaughter that she prayed for, who turned two the month before she died. She would never benefit from knowing her Nanna. These are my two children who are beginning lives of their own. My mom's face becomes harder and harder to see, and my memory of her sad life seems to be fading as time marches on.

If my mom would have lived, based on her rheumatoid arthritis alone, she would have been crippled and bedridden. As it was, her kidneys failed because of her diabetes. She was told by her doctor that she would never be a candidate for a kidney transplant. Dialysis would be in her future. She would die before that became a reality. When I stop to think of how horrible my mom's health was and how she must have felt every day, I shudder to think how I would have handled all that she had to deal with.

Although her poor health never improved, she still chose to be a mom to six children. I'm sure that she had options. I came to accept the reality that my mom could not meet my needs in most areas of my life. We simply lived together beneath the same roof. The tables can quickly turn and they did for me. I combed my mom's hair, massaged her feet, cleaned the house and cooked. I would be the one to take her to the doctor when she got older. Four out of six children lived out of town.

I still have the same questions: Did my mom lose hope in life itself? Did she hang on because she was responsible for raising her six children on her own? Where did her strength come from? Did she know how her children felt? Did she cry herself to sleep out of guilt, not being able to do any better as a mom?

She was a sick mom who wasn't afforded the necessities of life which otherwise would have made all the difference in the world. As it stood, living day after day against all hope, my mom was forced to simply give up in every way possible. She never expected anything from anyone. Did she realize that her life, though no fault of her own resulted in me having no hope that resulted in me being crippled on most levels?

Her circumstances are to blame, not her. My mom gave new meaning to being invisible while on this earth, which has left me with a profound respect for her, something that I unfortunately never really appreciated until many years after her death. I just want to thank her!

My mom gave me more than she possibly could have known when she gave me permission to go to church with Godly people whom she could trust. Those who picked me up for church every single week never seemed to tire of it. Many of them gave us a meal from time to time. They gave us bibles and taught us how to read it. More importantly, and unbeknownst to my mom was the opportunity she gave me to hear about the truth and love of the one true God of the Universe.

Years later I had the pleasure of taking my mom to church now and then when her health permitted. I had already shared with her the good news of Jesus Christ throughout my young life. Planting the good news of Jesus Christ in someone's heart is what God commands his believers to do, and he is faithful to bring that good news to fruition according to his Sovereignty. I experienced this personally.

My mom came to accept Jesus Christ as Lord and Savior over her life one year before God took her home. "Absent from the body and present with the Lord" 2 Corinthians 5:8 NIV consoles my very soul when I try to reconcile my mom's life on this earth. I know with certainty that she is safe in the arms of Jesus as I write these words. Her health failed her in all ways possible while she was on this earth. She is forever healed in heaven.

My mom gave me one nugget of advice on rearing a child. Tell them that you love them, she would say. She obviously had her own regrets. This helped to fill in one small gap as I grew to see the bigger picture. Always being the underdog, and everyone being better than me when I was growing up was hard to live out. My mom would convey to me months before she died that she was proud of me. Although it took nearly a life time, her few words of encouragement would speak volumes to me as I began to write my book.

I wanted my children to never to think that they are better than anyone else, never to leave others out, especially the underdog and never judge a book by its covering. Perhaps my unfortunate experiences had a silver lining after all.

My kids have little knowledge of just how my life as a child materialized and played out to the degree that it did. And unless they walk in my shoes, they will never be able to relate no matter how many stories I share about my personal experiences. I would rather they never relate, than to see them repeat my life as a young child.

All these years later, remembering vividly how hopeless and devoid I was, can still make my heart skip a beat. It has taken many years to play catch-up and yet I still find myself regularly seeking God to help me make sense of it all while trusting him to fill in my deep seeded voids.

Only a few are left who saw the path I had to walk while standing on the outside looking in. They can attest to a measure of what my life was truly about. I say this in one breath, and in the very next, I see clearly how invisible I was by my own omission. I was too embarrassed to ask for help. I wish that I had the tools to share with my Sunday School Teachers my deep hurts.

They didn't know everything I went through. They saw me from the outside, and some would say that is enough. They don't have any idea what I went through on the inside. I hid it well. I wasn't encouraged to share my feelings from my very start. Things were very different back in those days. People didn't share their feelings in those days in the way they do today. People were much more private.

We could use a little more privacy today. Children have gone from seen and not heard, to being thrown into an adult's world where they have no business being thrown into. Age appropriate isn't practiced by many today. That explains much in this generation. I, on the other hand wasn't shared vital information that would have made a huge difference in my life; that which could have permitted me from playing catch-up all my life. Today's young people are growing up too fast emotionally. Both ends of the spectrum can cripple.

I continue to grow in my walk with Jesus Christ. As I look back, I can say with confidence that regardless of my circumstances as a child; which I can now say was no fault of my own; my God heard my cry. My God opened my spiritual eyes to see his truth that has set me free for all eternity. My God bottled my tears. My God protected me from more than I am aware of. My God delivered me. My God saved my life emotionally, and physically over and over again. My God saved my soul.

My past circumstances, the deep hurts I endured, my immense sadness, my loneliness, and rejection by many has left me with voids that are unequivocally undeniable. That is what God in his goodness permitted me to go through, and my God walked right beside me through all those experiences. It would take me years to begin to see his hand of protection over me. God can and does take our frailty and our mistakes and makes us whole. He never leaves us or forsakes us. He continually grows us to become what he ordained the moment he created us. May I always this side of heaven give him all credit, all glory, all praise and all adoration for who he is in my life.

My many voids are the result of my unfortunate circumstances. Not having a leader in the family and having a very sick mom resulted in our poverty. God gives children a mom and a father for a reason. His design is perfect.

What does poverty look like, and in what ways does poverty hurt, cripple and paralyze? It was never about me and it was never my fault. It was about living in a fallen world, making wrong choices, and not knowing God personally, and with bad choices come consequences. And more times than not, we pay other's consequences. With that all to say, I will always be grateful that my prayers to God were answered in not taking my mom from me when I was a too young to comprehend.

CHAPTER 5

GEARING UP

1 Peter 1:13

Before my middle school years would come to an end and if such a thing were even possible, I would be reminded again how voided I was. How much more could I possibly endure? I go from having bad memories at middle school where I nearly had my hair set on fire, having boys chase me home, being bullied and constantly harassed, and treated poorly by teachers.

Now I am forced to ride a metro bus across town for the next four years to attend high school. Trying against all odds to forget my unfortunate experiences up to this point, would only make me more aware of the unknowns that I was not in the least prepared for.

Although entering high school was nothing special to me, I would soon learn that it was really special to other students. I attended class with most of the same kids who had gone to my middle school, seemingly with more money to spend, more bragging, cars, vacations, more memories of all sorts, and what my own children have experienced; some memorable fun times.

I would soon learn that there was something very different to the stories I was forced to listen to in middle school. The innocent sleepovers in middle school evolved into parties that didn't include parents at home in high school. Drugs, cigarettes and alcohol replaced popcorn, soda and a movie. Once again, I found yet another facet that prevented me from fitting in. Living a life of feel-good drugs, I was told to numb themselves, forgetting, and getting high just to get high was the new norm for these kids. I mean, I could have used some numbing and some much-needed forgetting. But the fact that I had no money, no car, and no friends shut that door.

I recall that a few of the students in my classes began to talk with me. I figured out months later that I was a good audience for them. In all fairness, they would share some of their snacks with me on occasion. Fortunately, as they planned their party's weekend after weekend, and sharing their experiences on Monday never caused me to envy that lifestyle. Perhaps it was lack of money.

A few students continued to ask me over to their houses, and I avoided them for weeks. First, I knew my mom would never allow me to go and therefore I never asked her. In this case, being afraid of my own shadow kept me from wanting to go. I attribute this to God protecting me. I knew this fact well, but for some reason I didn't rejoice in who I was as a believer. I just didn't participate in anything good or bad. I continue to see how profoundly empty I was.

My desperation to fit in could have made me an easy target for being used and abused regularly by those who made themselves believe that they were superior. My embarrassment about where I lived, my clothing, my hygiene and my lack of so many things was enough to keep me hidden away from others. I have thanked the Lord frequently for how he obviously protected me from so many unknowns, that I am still unaware of today. I am forced to say that it appears that God worked hard to protect me from myself. What other explanation could there be?

Government Jobs were provided for students of low income, who earned decent grades throughout their high school years. This helped in many ways. I was able to buy a few things that I had never had before. My mom required me to give her some money to help with the household expenses. Actually, we had free rent, food stamps, and free lunches at school. I obeyed.

I felt the loss of income more when I only worked in the office before school, during lunch, and during study hall. I remember clearly making $33 every two weeks and having to give my mom the same amount $10,00 each week that I gave her in the summer, leaving me with $13 for personal needs. I wanted my mom to escape poverty equal to me escaping. I wanted to give her even more. I wanted to erase her past. I dreamed of doing more for her to make her life easier. I felt helpless and at times hopeless. I would dream of a job that paid enough to get my mom out of government housing into her own home with her children before they grew up, so the guilt that she felt in how her children had to grow up could be erased from her mind.

Working in the high school office was on some level easier. It was definitely emotionally easier. The office staff were kind to me and appreciated my help. I was becoming a pretty good typist at this point, so they allowed me to type unimportant papers for them. My mom insisted that I take typing classes at school. It has served me well most of my life. I still had the same on-going desire to fit in. I worked very hard and was as invisible as I could be, as to not cause any stress, thereby jeopardizing my job. I needed this job badly, and I was relieved not to have to go through anymore hiring interviews.

The school was sponsoring its annual twenty-five-mile marathon to raise money for diabetes. I decided to give it a chance. My mom gave me the green light. I did it in honor of her living with diabetes. There were walkers and runners. The office staff encouraged me and supported me. After hours into the race, I quickly realized that my legs were no more prepared to run this long race than I was prepared for this society. I almost threw in the towel at one point as the cars would come by checking on the runners. Those who decided to stop did so without hesitation. I'm sure a healthy self-esteem played a part here.

Observing those who chose to stop tempted me not to finish as well. I would like to think that it was my sheer determination to finish, but the truth is I was embarrassed and based on how others treated me, I did my part in avoiding any additional humiliation that I had a measure of control of. I equally didn't want to disappoint the office staff who were cheering me on.

Back at my apartment with the race behind me, my legs would reveal to me a very different story about how leg muscles work after this level of exertion. Something that I didn't have the knowledge of thirty plus years ago. It would equally occur to me what the consequences of a 25-mile marathon would look and feel like 24 hours later. Well, needless to say, I found myself walking out the front door bowlegged to catch the bus for school. My mom was not a fan of allowing her kids to stay home from school. Thank goodness we didn't have the bubonic plague in our era. I'm really not kidding here.

The office at school had windows that were visible from the school grounds, and the staff saw me practically crawling to one of my classes. They asked why I didn't take advantage of staying home as some other students did. They obviously didn't know my mom.

Although some of the office staff apparently appreciated me, thinking I was worthy on some level, my fellow classmates didn't join them with that thought. I was constantly forced to hear all the joys of their lives and see it demonstrated in various ways. I would have felt better years later if I had found out that the stories about their lives were all false or at least exaggerated. I would soberly find out their actual lives were just as they claimed. Judging from the colleges some attended, this was confirmation that their lives continued to improve.

I would hear that some of the kids at school had part time jobs to put gas in the cars gifted to them by their parents. They always had what they needed and seemingly wanted. Our worlds were polar opposite.

Many fellow students wore braces on their teeth in high school. I never understood why groups of friends all had braces at the same time. I would see the end result and desired to wear them as well. I do recall a classmate who had a cracked front tooth. I was very concerned about her social life; afraid that people might reject her or make fun of her so I reached out to her to show my concern. I, on the other hand had crooked and chipped yellow teeth.

As I look back, I realize this is a prime example of how my voids, my deficits, and the rejection I experienced from others led me to accept what society had pegged for me. I came to accept the fact that I didn't fit in, and more times than not, I didn't belong. I allowed others to dictate my worth, and define me most of my life as a result of my unfortunate experiences that I had to endure. My personal consistencies have always equated to a big negative for me. No voice to defend, coupled with low self-esteem allowed some to disrespect me.

The pretty girls were liked by all the teachers, and those in charge would turn a blind eye to their disobedience. These girls would speak to me at times and their silliness made me laugh, but I envied the attention that the teachers gave to them and others, but somehow always excluded me. I recall a time when we were going to our next class, one of the silly girls grabbed my arm and told me that we were going to skip class. I attempted to get away, only to have her grip my arm more. The more I tried to escape her grip, the more she would laugh.

The late bell rang as the principle was walking by, but he ignored what she was doing. He just shook his head at her, with a smile made I add. She would be one of those pretty girls. She knew I was a rule follower, and getting to class after the tardy bell rang didn't represent me. She finally let go. My heart was already in my throat, now I have to open the closed door to my classroom. I didn't look up when I walked in. I saw more of the floor during those four years of high school than I did what was in front of me.

Not having a father in the house to guide, direct and lead, brought consequences that I didn't realize until years later. If I were blessed to have my mom's listening ear, I can imagine that I would have asked her questions, and shared with her how others treated me. Perhaps I would not have tolerated bad behavior directed at me. The only thing I had to go on was my personal consistencies. I was fully aware of my mom's expectations when I was in elementary school. Were her expectations of me the same in high school? She never said otherwise, so I acted and reacted the same with my classmates in middle, and high school as I did in those first six years of school.

My desperation to fit in should have steered me down the wrong path. Another example of Gods' protection. When my classmate treated me that way, it caused me to trust others even less. This girl was accustomed in getting her own way based on our principal's reaction to what she was doing to me. I was accustomed to getting bad behavior by those who knew I was an easy target. I would learn early in life that consistency whether good or bad, or in my case horrid, each one of us will live out our own reality.

Because I did not have the needed tools to fit in emotionally, socially, or otherwise, I became invisible and self-protective. Never having any expectations in life can result in one finding themselves floating on air at the prospect of having a wonderful time, only to be failed time and time again. Being teased at school by kids was one thing. Being teased by those adults whose word couldn't be trusted later in life was quite another. They both hurt. The latter left scars.

Instead of someone out there taking the chance to develop a friendship with me by giving me a mere chance, I was consistently judged by their standards. I was somehow always reminded who I was in my little world by others. I would dream of finding one person who could make a difference in my life and potentially change the direction of my life.

By offering a measure of kindness that might seem insignificant to you, could perhaps change the life of a person who feels totally lost without hope. I remind myself that my classmates were children just like me. When one grows up and revisits their past, the pain for some can be so bad that you refuse to visit it again, or you do something about the clarity you have now, and with that comes healing.

I wish that I had the needed tools back then that would have prevented so much pain. The level of pain that unfortunately shapes your way of thinking and your way of doing things. Your left with the idea that perhaps you will never truly know who God created you to be. Your God given abilities never play out the way they were designed to play out.

Falling behind in every stage of development keeps you behind. Time doesn't stand still, and before you know it, you find yourself so lost, so voided and so far behind that there doesn't seem to be a chance for catching up. These scars never seem to heal and without anyone to protect you, society uses it against you in countless ways.

If things never change, such people are left ill-equipped, and the consequences are devastating. Falling behind at any stage of development can start a spiraling-down effect that sets up a child for failure. They spend the rest of their life playing catch-up. Society judges you, defines and classifies you.

I would soon discover that having so many voids in my life, the result of all the hurt, pain, and rejections that I endured, allowed no room for my contentment. So, although I would love the occasional pack of gum or ice-cream cone, it would prove itself to be a reminder that such things were never going to be normal in my life. Quite different when I was a young girl with the opportunity to go to camp. I was eight. Kids have hope when they are only eight years old. They aren't emotionally mature enough to comprehend the injustices of society.

I realized later in life that my attitude wasn't one of ingratitude; it was about being profoundly devoid emotionally, psychologically, and mentally. Those vital tools that are needed in every stage of development, is a matter of succeeding in every area of your life, or failing in every area of your life. My lack of tools kept me paralyzed.

Even though there were far too many times to count when God seemed to be very distant from me, my God knew me. Many years later, I would begin to process this knowledge and put it somewhat into perspective. My God was fully aware of my circumstances. He saw my extraordinary pain and how I was rejected and treated by others. He was aware of my low self-esteem, my legitimate needs, and my genuine desire for guidance and direction in my life. He knew of my hunger for knowledge, and my unawareness in my own little world. Because God knows all things, he knew my needs were never met.

Through it all my God protected me. I just had to grow up to see this truth. He was preparing me to see my need for him and him alone. It has been life-changing. The seed was planted when my mom allowed me to go to church where there were true born-again bought by the precious blood of Jesus Christ believers, who would pour into my life the truth of God's word, which would manifest itself in me and begin to mold me into who I am this very day. My God protected me numerous times from emotionally dying, to the point of no return.

I would read my bible at times having no clue what it said. I memorized bible verses for a reward; gum. I even took my bible to school. I couldn't comprehend any of it, but I wanted to obey my God. I had learned along my journey that we must not ask

God why. We do, and I did, but as I have grown, I see that God is in control, no matter what. He is omnipresent, omnipotent, and omniscient.

He does allow certain things to happen. We live in a fallen world which manifests itself in many, many ways. Our own choices can make us or break us. For me living in a fallen world makes total sense, and for me personally belonging to Jesus Christ makes even more sense, because of his mercy in choosing me, a sinner saved by his grace.

God doesn't allow us to go through anything we can't handle, and he makes a way out for us according to his Sovereignty. I have come to think at times *Wow! he must have thought that I was a tower of pure strength.* I wouldn't know. I gave up long ago. I became invisible; I became numb; I simply had no fight in me. As I understand it now, my mom's acceptance of what life seemed to measure out to her became my own acceptance of what life measured out to me.

From my experiences along my journey, I believe that God restores, heals and blesses beyond measure. God's promise never to leave us or forsake us is written in stone. I can attest to this on a personal level. God's peace which surpasses all understanding would become incredibly real in my life as I began to live it out. I couldn't see it when I was in the midst of my pain as a clueless little girl who grew up impoverished. I had to get to the other side to believe that I was never responsible for how I had to live.

Perhaps the unfortunate hard-core facts that presented themselves in my growing-up years that forced me to look at the reality of my life marked by poverty on every level, overshadowed the most important truth, Gods' truth.

Although I believed that God loved me, after all he loves everyone, and that has to include me, perhaps I subconsciously made the lives of others superior to mine. And the fact that I couldn't relate to them or obtain what they had eventually led me to conclude that I was less than they were, so much less that it profoundly paralyzed me on all levels, which allowed fear to set in and own me for most of my life.

Although God allows us to go through things that are most unpleasant, which can at times make us feel as if we will die in the midst of them, he is always in arm's length of us. Our God-given free Will has the potential to cause each of us to grow into the person God has designed us to, according to his Sovereignty, or else we can use our free Will to depend on ourselves. The end result will be regret if we choose the lateral. Trusting him wholeheartedly would begin to prove itself nearly a lifetime later.

"I know the plans I have for you,' declares the Lord, 'plans to prosper, and not to harm you, plans to give you hope and a future" Jeremiah 29:11 NIV. Living in a fallen world is a reality. Having God to guide, and direct our paths is also a reality. Trusting God with my soul seemed to be one thing, and finding myself trusting God with me physically was quite another.

The positions I found myself in at times, would be overwhelming. Trusting God at times when I didn't see him was equally overwhelming. Those who seemed to want to hurt me caused me to question God's protection over me, resulting in me wanting to throw my trust out the window. That was just another area in my life that I shut down in. I expected someone to hurt me and like a sitting duck, it wasn't a matter of "if", it was a matter of "when".

I remember my mom having to go into a very rough neighborhood at times to see a particular doctor, and I would go with her. Panic would overwhelm me, however, I always managed to keep my fears from my mom. We drove up to get as close to the office as possible. As she was getting out of the car, her legs gave out and she slowly went down on the curb. A man came over and picked her up. He just looked at me as my mom walked into the building. My mom needed me and I just stayed in the car. I allowed my fear to fail my mom.

I locked the car doors and waited for her to come out from the Doctors office. I was numb. I was no more prepared to defend her or myself that day. The wait seemed endless. She finally came out and I tried to hide my emotions. I absolutely did not want her to know of all my fears. Perhaps if she had known, she would have owned them, and I couldn't handle that. My life at this point was polar opposite to hers in my health alone. I don't have the audacity to blame her or hold her accountable for how my life played out as a child. I unfortunately carried those real fears into my adulthood. Those fears that kept me silent when I was a child, were the same fears that kept me silent as an adult when I was raising my children.

Years later, I would discover that God was beginning to deliver me of some of my fears when I found myself not checking closets, doors or windows. I began to feel liberated. The confidence that nothing will ever happen to me according to his Sovereignty is true peace. What prevented me from reaching out to God for deliverance when I was a child?

I am astonished of how one's childhood experiences can affect, define, and control every area of your life, and come right alongside into adulthood when you least expect it.

My mom brought much of how she was raised into her adult life as well, with the exception of alcohol. My mom wouldn't allow a drop of alcohol into her apartment ever. I respect that strength in her as I look back. She was proactive in doing her part in breaking at least one cycle. I appreciate my mom's strength more now that I am far removed from my childhood.

It stands to reason why children aren't emotionally equipped for the adult world. Some of my mom's voids would explain much to me nearly a lifetime later. Wounded people can't operate in the same way emotionally as healthy people can, anymore, then a new believer can teach the bible in quite the same way as a seasoned Saint can.

The difference of being born with a silver spoon in one's mouth verses being born in poverty, is that both carry its own responsibilities in life. No one is exempt from the needed awareness of their own world. Opinions based on personal experiences are quite different based on the lens one has been looking through.

Being born into poverty carries no blame for the helpless innocent child, but it does bring with it; its own challenges. A person looking through the lens of poverty will see things much differently, then those born with a silver spoon see through their lens. The two worlds, rich and poor are polar opposite of each other. However, the end result of each has much to do with how a person responds to his or her personal situation. This is where the end result can be reversed. Many areas in my life have been reversed because of God and him alone.

It is no more the credit of those born with a silver spoon in their mouths than it is the fault of those born in poverty. If we could see the bigger picture more clearly, perhaps we could all be part of the solution, instead of being so divided, based on each one's interpretations.

It's what you do with what you have been given that ultimately matters. The difference here is that God looks at the heart and judges fairly, while mankind looks at the outward appearance and judges unfairly.

If I would judge my mom for all that occurred in my life, I would be guilty of judging her in the same way as the world judges. She said enough to me that paints a clearer picture of her heart. She had regrets. She would have done things differently if she could have. She wasn't in control of her health. She would get bad news every time she went to the doctor. Her body was so saturated with pharmaceutical drugs. She also had many adverse reactions to these pharmaceutical drugs that were prescribed in the hope of keeping her alive. My mom was a guinea-pig for the doctors.

My mom never knew of my hurts and fears as a child. She didn't live long enough to see how my childhood fears played out in my young adult years. She never knew how my fears increased when I became a mom. She never knew that I was afraid that my kids may taste a portion of what I lived through. I worked as hard in not transferring my fears to my kids as I did in protecting my mom from seeing my fears as a young child growing up in government housing.

My kids have no idea just how voided my life was growing up. God giving me a life polar opposite to my moms' life was such a blessing to me that I did not want them to know how pitiful my life was as a child. I was never given permission to validate my countless voids growing up, and I didn't want to burden my kids with how my life played out. I thought perhaps my kids would be affected emotionally. I didn't want the guilt that I took on as a child to transfer onto them.

I thanked God regularly for allowing me to be a mom and for permitting me to be healthy enough to do for my kids what my mom simply had no chance of doing. I was determined to fill every single void in my children that wasn't filled in me. I desperately wanted them to know the love of Jesus.

They can never say that they weren't told the truth of Gods' word. They may say that I went overboard at times, praying too long before meals, and before bed at times. Will they ever see that those efforts were the result of my undying love for them? I still recall my son asking if I could pray quickly for meals at times with a smile on his face, because he was starving to death, all relative.

I was a volunteer at school to show my kids the importance of education. I worked side by side with teachers. I was the room mom, the book fair coordinator, the school party organizer, the PTA vice president, and the chaperone on field trips to name just a few. I would treat other children like my own when we went on field trips if their moms had to work. I knew what it felt like to be left out and my conscience would work over time in reminding me.

I endlessly cooked; entertained my kids' friends; read my kids a great many books; facilitated many art projects; birthday parties; and outings; joined them in roller-skating; biking; and hiking; involved them in sports and music lessons; talked endlessly with them; involved them in church activities of all sorts, camps, and youth retreats; every single thing that my poor mom had no chance of doing, as the result of her many illnesses.

What I was forced to see at times, was that I was filling *my* voids in my kids' lives not *theirs*. I picked them up before they fell. They lived a life equally as enriched, if not more so than any kid with whom I went to school with. Actually, they lived a life far superior to the lives of all those kids as a result of being taught the good news of Jesus Christ. Everyone has their own voids, but I poured into them my love for them. Without that effort, I would have ceased to exist.

I hold my mom in the highest regard because I have never walked in her shoes or have been plagued by her bad health. Her illnesses destroyed her from the inside out.

By God's abundant mercy and grace, I have never been on a pharmaceutical drug in my life. I don't have diabetes as my mom. I have healthy lungs, and I can garden, play tennis, golf, and can walk for miles. I simply don't understand why at times my mom had to live the life she did. I do not blame God for my devoid life growing up. I choose to thank him for delivering me, and I earnestly pray that he uses me according to his Sovereign Will.

When voids are a normal way of life, catching up is virtually impossible. The scars begin to form, and the continual voids will begin to stunt the emotional, social, and physiological growth of the child. Such children are left to fend for themselves in a school setting where they aren't protected, and more times than not are thrown into adulthood ill-equipped and unprepared.

I know who I was in Christ long ago. I am now growing mightily in my walk with the Lord Jesus. It has taken me a long time to make sense of all that I have had to endure over the course of my life with the experiences I had as a child. I am now more equipped to comprehend it on a level that permits me to call it what it was.

I am an example of the unfortunate things that can happen in life, that is no fault of your own. I am also aware that growing up voided doesn't have as much to do with poverty as I thought. Being devoid of the critical tools needed in a young child's life will result in irreversible damage. Following behind in every stage of development is crippling. The end result is being abused by society in ways that not only takes one back to the hurt you experience as an innocent child, but begins a wound in adulthood that never seems to heal.

To not fit in and be excluded in your own little world as a result of endless voids creates deficits in one's life that paralyzes. Having to play catch-up results in constant failure on all levels. These voids follow you into adulthood with the same hurts and rejections by others on a much larger scale.

Not having a father, grandparents or an extended family seems to me to be the missing link. My mom and her children would have benefited greatly if we had what God intended for each of us to have in terms of a family. Stating the obvious seems so hopeful. Not ever experiencing it screams loud and clear its reality.

Being bullied by those who would see you as weak and unimportant as a child is painful. This instills fear into those who have no voice at home or at school. Most bullies are insecure and have their own set of issues stemming from their home life as well. They themselves are as wounded, as those whom they wound. Unfortunately, I didn't know this when I was a child.

However, in recognizing that bullies have issues, isn't the same as having voids so deep that you can't function in a society that demands certain behavior to be socially accepted and recognized. Most kids that are bullied don't grow up ill equipped to the degree that they can't be productive citizens. Life just moves on for them.

Kids whose vital and critical needs aren't met in any stage of development never catch up. They are seen as weak and unimportant. They are ostracized by some, treated poorly by others. Those who purposely ignore them, or look right through them secures their destiny to be left ill-equipped in society.

CHAPTER 6

SIMILARITY'S

Deuteronomy 31:6

Unbeknownst to me during my life as a child, God would be preparing me to volunteer in the inner city when I grew up. He would open the door for me to work with kids who lived in the inner city. What I would discover would be eye opening for me. I could personally relate to those who had so much less than others. They lived without a father in the home as well.

There were those who were poverty-stricken like me. One extraordinary discovery I would make was although these children were poor, and although I would discover various voids in them, they were more fortunate than I was as a child. They had new clothes, their hair was professionally done, they had jewelry, they went on outings, and they seemed to have money when needed. They celebrated their birthdays and received presents. They had healthy moms. There were times when I personally struggled with these facts.

God obviously permitted me to endure this challenge. Something I didn't sign up for. Some of these children with whom I ministered to on several levels thought I was born with a silver spoon in my mouth. They assumed that the color of my skin classified me as rich. Could they ever comprehend the truth of my life growing up?

We had a great relationship and were involved in many things together. These children represented fifty children who were part of a Christian dance team that performed at local churches. I have fond memories of working with these children. The dance instructor was endlessly devoted to them on a spiritual level. They were taught the love of Christ in every facet of their lives, including dancing, singing, and performing in front of many churches who supported this ministry, called the "God Squad." The leader was the choreographer, and wrote the lyrics of the Christian rap music that they would sing. The lyrics glorified God.

He would spend his days ministering to the kids through Bible study, playing sports, and teaching them the love of Christ. His right-hand helper opened her home regularly so the love of Christ could be poured into these children. I was extremely blessed to be a part of it. We would spend every Friday evening together. We had weekly bible studies. Transporting them to various Christian Camps each summer were a big hit for these young people.

The dreaded day would come when one of the girls needed to be taken home. I had taken kids to their apartments in different parts of Cincinnati. She just happened to live in the government-subsidized neighborhood that I had grown up in. My heart sank. I simply couldn't do it. I declined to drive her home without another adult present. The emotional state I was in didn't allow me to drive.

From their perspective, my life was so much better as a result of the color of my skin and where I now lived. I addressed it when the topic came up throughout our years together. I would be forced to prove to these girls that I was not born with a silver spoon in my mouth, not even a plastic spoon to make my point.

I finally shared with these girls where I grew up. After the shock wore off, they still didn't believe me until I told them my precise address and described the neighborhood. What a wake-up call that was for them. It was a wake-up call for me as well for a much different reason. I didn't choose to share with them where I grew up because I didn't want to connect myself to something that left me a shell of a person. Out of sight, out of mind. God obviously called me to work with these children and going back to my neighborhood for a brief moment was in his plan as well.

It just explains where I was emotionally in some respects. A fear that I may have to go back there petrified me. These girls knew that I wasn't rich based on material things, they just assumed as we all do at times. We never had any issues with each other's nationality.

I soon found myself accompanying the girls' home with the other leader. As we were driving down the well-known street that is forever etched in my mind, my stomach flip-flopped! My life flashed before my eyes, and I experienced that numb feeling that had been such a large part of my growing-up years. As I see it now, I apparently had to revisit my neighborhood to appreciate what God began to do in my life as a child, that I never realized. My focus was on the here and the now. My past didn't apply to the "good old days". There wasn't anything pleasant or better about my life as a child compared to my life as a young adult. In saying that, I would begin to see what God was preparing for me in my future. Working with these inner-city children was in Gods' plan for me. These girls would learn a valuable lesson in not judging a book by its cover before you gain the facts.

The kids that I worked with actually had many more opportunities than my family could have ever dreamt of. We were the minority, as one of the very few Caucasian families living among the African Americans in those days. They have more government programs with more awareness of what life is like for the impoverished today than they did when I was a child. I loved those inner-city kids, and I felt it an honor to be in their company. They have no idea that although we had similarity's, we had more differences, and those differences were in their favor, not mine. However, we had tons of fun; sleepovers, parties, cooking, movies, activities, and trips that were supported by local churches. I pray that I was a testimony in how God can take the broken pieces of our lives and make them whole.

The night I drove past the apartment that I had called home for nearly 18 years was necessary in showing me how God takes care of his own. This would be the beginning of what God would reveal to me, and it has taken years and years for me to see the bigger picture. I stand in awe as I continue to realize just how much my God has covered me with his hand of protection, and has walked with me through those difficult times when I was a child. Of this I am confident.

I continue to see more clearly how God is working through me, using my childhood experiences to reach out to others, to give them the hope in Jesus that I had; even when my circumstances didn't make a bit of sense. When you can't see it, the hopelessness begins to set in, and when nothing seems to change for the better, you shut down and give up. God gave me the ability and the enthusiasm to love on those children in the inner city and pour into them the love of Jesus Christ. As I continue to look back, I see how God used me in the inner city as an adult. I would begin to realize just how much I was beginning to grow emotionally.

A much different story in how unprepared and clueless I was when my mom needed me the most in a nursing home over the last months of her life. Having no tools can and will cripple you when you are needed most. Years later when I began to awaken emotionally, thoughts would begin to come to my mind causing me to reminisce about my mom's life. I was forced to come to the realization that I had no more skills in meeting my mom's emotional needs, anymore, than she had in meeting mine over those informative years.

To state that I gave my all can seem so cliché. In some ways it covers up the truth; a smokescreen to the reality that one is hiding behind, which one doesn't want exposed. Her doctor conveyed to me that unless I was a nurse and available 24/7, I would not be able to meet her needs physically. This truth would not lessen the guilt that can flood over me at times when I least expect it.

Although I would nurse my mom back to health in her out-patient surgery's, I would never be successful in meeting her emotional needs. Our outings were keeping up with her doctor appointments. Transporting her to appointments would always be in silence. I live with the regret of not being better prepared, and more equipped to meet her needs on a deeper level. I simply shut down emotionally.

Perhaps I did for her what I deemed necessary and what I wanted. Having a void seemingly filled with tangible things simply made life easier. Looking back causes me to see that she wanted more from me. I shared with her a portion of what I had. I wanted her to experience what I thought would complete her and make her "normal." Those things that I thought would complete me and make me "normal" You can only give what you have.

Marrying young in an attempt to escape a life of poverty is a constant reminder of living a life ill-equipped. I found myself living and existing, similar to how I lived as a child. I hid my deep disappointments well when I was married. I had found someone to give me attention that would unfortunately begin a life of strings attached that would plague me for most of my life. An insecure person devoid on all levels, a nobody just trying to escape a life of poverty.

I had no clue what life was about, so to find myself jumping blindly into a marriage designed for two adults embarking on a life together gave new meaning to being unprepared. Absolutely void of all the necessary tools to move forward as husband and wife. Two individuals who aren't prepared in the slightest to handle life's decisions is ludicrous. I can attest to this on a personal level.

As life moved on whether I was ready or not, I would find myself going forward with my ongoing personal experiences, amid the new struggles that although looked much different from those of my childhood, would rear its ugly head at times and be a constant reminder of how voided I was.

For me playing catch-up in all areas of my life, emotional, psychological, and even physical has made my journey through life much more challenging than it had to be. To give myself permission to have high expectations has been a balancing act for me. I vacillate between not feeling guilty about it and being prideful.

God continues to heal me from the inside out. I give him all the credit for opening the door for me to tell my story. It took such a long time for me to complete it because my memories of how I had to grow up were simply too painful. I couldn't seem to get my thoughts together at times, and relive the horrible pain that I had to go through just to survive. And life just got in the way. To relive those memories and raise my children at the same time wasn't possible. I allowed nothing to get in the way of me pouring into their lives that which was not poured into mine.

Although my life as an adult was polar opposite to what it was as a child, I did have a measure of the same fear that my children may experience my life on some level. This would terrify me. I continually thank God for is grace in how he has taken such good care for my kids throughout these years in a personal way. He has blessed us with the needed funds. He has blessed us with good health. He has blessed me to pour into them the hope they can have in trusting Jesus alone in all circumstances.

God continues to give me the needed hope that I will reign with Christ Jesus for all eternity because of what he did for me, and continues to do in me. I am fully aware that God will never leave me or forsake me. He has more than proven that over the course of my life. I am fully aware that I am unconditionally loved, chosen and precious in God's eyes. I am fully aware that my circumstances as a child growing up in poverty were not poured out on me by God. I am fully aware that God uses our weaknesses and our circumstances to grow us closer to him.

Being on the other side of all my childhood experiences has given me all the hope I need this side of heaven. This "hope" that others had never seemed to include me. I would learn that this life on this earth is a blink of an eye compared to eternity. All pain, sadness, hurt, disappointments, unkindness, and rejection by others, as the result of sin will cease when we get to Heaven.

I'm finding the more I grow in my walk with the Lord, my unfortunate life experiences have been an extraordinarily small price to pay in exchange for the knowledge that I will reign with Christ for all eternity, not because of anything that I did, could do, work for, or especially deserve. Only God can open our spiritual eyes to see the truth of who Jesus Christ is. His free gift of salvation is available to all who simply respond to his call by faith and believe. That includes me.

Those chosen by society never seemed to include me. I was unequivocally chosen before the foundation of the world by the one true God of the Universe. I am now free; free to not to be a slave to sin, free to accept who I am in Christ Jesus, free to witness the good news of Jesus Christ, free to be part of the Great Commission, and free from all the worlds worries and fears of the unknown which plagued me for most of my life as an innocent, naive, and emotionally unhealthy young girl.

I knew precisely what it felt like to be categorically rejected, to be completely alone, and to be void of all good things. I equally know what it feels like to belong to the KING of all kings and LORD of all lords.

The concept of all things working together for my good is an element of my personal growth making me to be more like Jesus Christ. It is key to me having a deeper love for Jesus, with the confidence that I belong to God, and I can trust in him alone for my mere existence. The horrendous pain I felt in my childhood and into my adulthood that was meant for evil in my life is being turned around for my good and for God's ultimate glory Romans 8:28.

Never experiencing unconditional love from anyone keeps you stuck emotionally. As my life became a consistency of unfilled voids, I simply shut down thereby diminishing any chance of things ever changing for the better for me.

I will never know all that my mom had to endure when she was a child. By the time she shed a mere glimpse of light on her life as a child, I was already crippled. I know enough to say that her choices were slim to none. She never seemed to escape her childhood to the degree as I did. My mom arrived into adulthood already married. She never had the chance to grow up in any area. She would carry those unfilled voids into her life and just make the best of it. She would turn around one day with six kids to feed and clothe. She moved forward ready or not. She did without to give what little she had to her children.

The government helped those families that were impoverished. Government housing, food stamps and medical treatments would define my mom raising six children on her own. When I think back on how she managed with what little she had, and how she would make her funds last absolutely amazes me. I would have to grow up and look back to see how incredible she was with that responsibility. Although we didn't have the food that my kids have been blessed with, my mom made dishes that were substantial and filled us up, well, for those who would eat it.

I wasn't made aware that real milk was liquid until years later. I wasn't a fan of "real" milk either. The milk we had was made from some white powder and water added to disguise what it was. It didn't work. Puffed-wheat cereal, thick government bologna, beanie weenies, government cheese, and yucky white bread were all staples in my life as a child, and I fought eating them every step of the way. I simply could not eat. I would quickly learn that the disappointments of food would be the norm for me, equal to the many teases I endured. Unbeknownst to me at the time would be what was in store for me, that followed me along my life's journey. The many teases would cause me to not trust people because the end result was always the same; disappointment.

My mom had her way of knowing when I had gone too long without eating. She would fry potatoes frequently. Now that would be a favorable definition of consistency in my life. I must take responsibility for being hungry at times due to my distaste for our food choices.

As I go back in time and attempt to look into my childhood, my purpose is to gain understanding. It helps me to answer the many why's, and how's, which is what helps me to make sense of it all today.

CHAPTER 7

PERSPECTIVE

Matthew 5:14

I would learn a new definition of hunger as I began to learn about the world in which I lived. I would see the bigger picture of Third World Hunger compared to my concept of hunger. I gained knowledge by reading about it. Having the opportunity to visit a Third World Country would affect me more than any literature could ever explain.

Supporting a Third World Country in a small way has been rewarding. I would continue to see the meaning of hunger on a different level, and I will never forget it this side of heaven.

There is hunger and there is *hunger* as I would soon find out. Although going to bed hungry and staying hungry at times was as real in my life as breathing. I was finally able to put it into perspective.

I would have the opportunity to go to an orphanage in Guatemala years later, an experience that would bless me and touch me in ways that would turn out to be life-changing. The orphanage was run by Godly people. The children were loved and cherished and most importantly they were taught daily the love of Jesus Christ. We were a team of about thirty. Our mission was to help with the needed maintenance, including painting the dorms. We brought tennis shoes for the children representing "Samaritan's Feet". We washed their feet and put new shoes on them. They were overjoyed with huge smiles on their faces that would bring tears to our eyes.

We interacted with these children in playing outdoor games, socializing and getting to know them on a personal level. This orphanage sat up on a mountain with barbed wire fencing around the compound. The property was impeccably cared for. The love of Christ saturated that place. There were missionary doctors and dentists who took care of these children. I was most impressed by the fact that most of these kids had huge smiles on their faces. Their hair was cut and fixed the way they wanted. Their teeth were beautiful. They could have been taken out of Guatemala and placed in a mansion, and no one would have known that they weren't born with a silver spoon in their mouths. They had their own identities. They were made to share, but each had one possession that others needed permission to touch. These kids were very secure.

These children whose parents gave them up had no idea how other people lived outside the walls of this orphanage. Many who were infants when they came to the orphanage would have no idea what the condition of their parent's home life was like in the different cities in Guatemala. They had no idea that they were really poor. They had nothing to compare it with. They were hygienically clean. There clothes were laundered. They had proper nutrition, simple foods, but nutritious. They each had a bed to sleep in with clean sheets, a pillow, and blankets. The Den Moms adored them and conveyed that to them in every way possible.

This orphanage had a hospital for renal patients as a result of those living with diabetes. Parents would drop them off without permission stating that if the orphanage didn't take them, they would die in their arms. The had no insurance, and no outlets. Missionary doctors would visit on a regular basis, assisting the doctors who lived at the orphanage. Those children who needed kidney transplants would unfortunately die as the result of not having donors. It was extremely hard to watch. It was very humbling to meet the medical team who had worked there for years; those who poured their time and love into these precious children. We were permitted to visit the hospital on occasion, and those children I met were all smiles. Some were sicker than others, but they all had such life in their faces. Those who simply had no hope short of a miracle from God were confident that they would be healed when God took them home.

The children's days began with reading Gods' word and prayer, and ended the same way. They were spoken too, and equally listened too. They talked about the love of God, and were taught what the bible says about his free gift of Salvation. They were taught to be confident in who they were in Christ Jesus after truly coming to faith in Jesus alone.

They were treated kindly by all adults in the orphanage who showed no favoritism or unfair treatment. They experienced no rejection. No one ostracized them. They were delighted to sing for us about the love of Jesus Christ in their own language. They would quickly learn that I could braid hair. Gorgeous braids filled that place. We would learn that some of the orphans became Den moms themselves when they grew up, a testimony to how God had rescued them from a life so dreadful in certain parts of Guatemala. I was blessed to get to know them and learn about their lives.

I can't relate to being given up by a parent. I can't relate to growing up in an orphanage. I can't relate to living in a Third World Country. I equally can't relate to this kind of unconditional love, acceptance, and attention. Having clean sheets and a pillow, having one's hair fixed, practicing good hygiene, ongoing communication, feeling safe, and permission to express oneself; I couldn't relate to any of these things.

These 500 children were protected from those who could hurt them, and those who had hurt them. They were spared the crippling that comes from being so voided that causes a person to become ill-equipped in a society for which he or she was created to be in. These children will one day know just how blessed they are to have been surrounded by people who loved them because they loved Jesus Christ. They were given the tools that are needed to grow in every stage of development. They have a chance to heal emotionally as a result of the unconditional love that God showed through those affiliated with this orphanage.

They all have similar experiences as to why they grew up in an Orphanage. I'm sure as they grow, they will have questions about their birth parents. I'm sure there will be different ways each one of these children deal with being raised by someone other than their biological parents. They deserve the needed validation as they process all that their lives entailed. Voids in one's life will manifest itself differently from person to person as a result of their own personal experiences. They are voids never-the-less. I can attest to this on a personal level.

When our team of 30 arrived in Guatemala, we found ourselves shocked at the level of poverty we saw. Pot holes were so large that a small car could fall in and never be seen again. Black smoke pouring out of the pipes, making it apparent that Vehicle Emissions was not a practice in Guatemala. When we were washing the feet of these children, I would ask my translator to apologize to the children that the water was so cold. He would tell me that they aren't accustomed to having warm water to bathe in. Just another example of how ignorance can plague those of us who have no clue how others live out their lives. Raw meat was hanging from the ceilings in the meat markets with a host of flies so large that you could see their facial features. One of the tour guides warned us not to buy their meat. He said only Guatemalans can safely eat this meat and other raw foods. We didn't need to be told twice.

This would begin a conversation of how blessed we are to live in America, and spoke about how much we take for granted. We are equally as ignorant about life in Guatemala as they are about life in America.

I began thinking how ignorance can define us all on some level. Many privileged in the United States are profoundly ignorant of things, but would never admit it. The innumerable opportunities, the overwhelming pleasures of life, the continual and changing technologies, and everything in between has blinded our society to such a degree that people aren't even aware that their lives are as voided as many who weren't afforded those pleasures in life. It just manifests itself differently.

Their voids are masked by material things that doesn't reveal itself until the pleasures and allures of this world cease to fulfill, eventually bringing on the same crippling paralysis that I endured as a young person; for a different reason, and on a profoundly different level. They are left to figure things out on their own as a result of being independent of God.

The children in the orphanage didn't have any bells and whistles that was noticeable. They had what matters most, the love of God. The city and villages in Guatemala screamed poverty. However, the landscape of Guatemala was breath taking. We stood in awe as we looked at the mountains. The beauty in the sky at any time of the day displayed Gods' amazing handiwork.

The children in the orphanage emulated Jesus well. They put us first. They treated us like we were special. This was very uncomfortable for me personally because I am not accustomed to being put above anyone. I wanted to serve them. I went there to work and meet their needs in tangible ways. There kindness was overwhelming. They welcomed us with open arms. They acted like we were better. Another uncomfortable feeling.

With each meal that we prepared for ourselves of the foods that were given to us, would be a constant reminder of what those children ate each and every day. Beans, rice, and a small piece of meat was the staple. We were blessed with foods that weren't much different than what we eat in America. I wonder if the verse that says the "last shall be first and the first shall be last" would disqualify most in America. God permitting me to go to Guatemala taught me much.

Helping others has always been rewarding to me. As I look back, I can see that helping others was not for personal gain. Those whom I helped had nothing to give back. Whether it was combing my neighbor's hair, massaging her arms, hanging out her clothes to dry, or just sitting with her seemed to come natural to me. My neighbor seemed to be the oldest person in our housing development. She was all alone.

As usual I would never gain any knowledge about her on a personal level. She needed help, and I enjoyed helping her. I give my mom credit for this to some degree. She helped others in simple terms. There were those who had more to give than my mom had. When I compare the two, I conclude that she gave more because it was truly a portion of all she had.

This situation in helping my elderly neighbor was much different in that I didn't do it to get her approval or her acceptance. She really needed me. Most of my acts of kindness when I became an adult was done to gain approval; to avoid the consistent rejection that I was accustomed to. I regret that I depended on mankind to the degree in which I did. I just wanted to be accepted even if I were deemed less. My expectations were low. Having a measure of contentment in the simple things in life served me well. I found very little to fill my voids as a child. Helping others took the camera off me.

God knew what he was doing when he orchestrated my steps that led to me working with children in the inner city. It wasn't about me. It was about God working through me to help others, that would begin to tell me a different story years later. He was showing me my willingness to help others was a gift he personally gave to me. I would begin experiencing that it is more blessed to give then to receive. I was taught this at church, but could never relate to its meaning until I grew up. Those things I gained monetarily when I grew would bring its real meaning to me on a personal level.

I would continue to teach children along my life's journey on many fronts. I would entertain young people in my kitchen teaching them to cook. Making cupcakes, breads and cookies and sharing them with others was a teachable moment. Seeing their eyes light up when they would learn that mixing colors together makes other colors. Making homemade playdough was a fond memory for them. Little things in life that brings a smile on a child's face is priceless in a world that seems to put money above all else. Reading to them or having school at my home was a hit for these children. I would get as much out of it as the children did. Those memories that wasn't afforded to me when I was a young child has benefited many, nearly a lifetime later. The kind of blessings that are given by God himself.

CHAPTER 8

MEMORIES

John 14:26

I would find myself working as a counselor at camp when my children were old enough to go to camp. And yes, my children attended the very camp that I went to as a child, although their experiences were very different from mine to say the least! Their clothes were clean and folded in a 'suitcase'. They had the needed notebook, pencils, markers, and toiletries equally to what their fellow campers had. They could swim, ride bikes, participate in the sporting events and more. They had the needed confidence to be part of whatever transpired at camp each summer. They would have no idea what this would mean to me from my perspective. They were just like all the other campers having a blast at camp. I still thank the Lord that my children didn't have to live out their young lives equal to mine. I worked hard to give them all the tools that I was aware of; to take them from one stage of development to the next stage of development, filling all gaps along the way. They will never truly understand to the fullest what went on inside my head and heart in reference to them. The silence I was forced to live out as a child, and the silence that I chose to live out to protect my children can't be quantified.

There were a few kids at camp who were similar to the socioeconomic status as I was. I now look for that one person to whom I can relate to in terms of having needs. Perhaps I am more sensitive in spotting that one person for the obvious. I have been blessed to help those in need without making it a public affair. To personally turn a blind eye or a deaf ear to such a person with whom I can personally relate too, would make it a worse offense than what I was forced to endure.

I think if children had more awareness when things just don't make sense in their lives, it would minimize the pain that they go through. Looking back; if I knew then what I would learn later in life, I could have been spared so much heartache that resulted in me giving up in life. If I was convinced that life could get better when I grew up, I can imagine that I would have had a measure of hope.

That which my mom was forced to live out had no chance of not pouring over to her children. This must have broken her heart at times. She must have taken some responsibility for that; after all she was the one who brought us into the world. And I personally knew a piece of her heart. She has been in the presence of Jesus for nearly thirty years now. She wouldn't choose to come back if she had the opportunity. And I wouldn't ask her to come back if given the choice. To do so would be the epitome of selfishness on my part.

Based on how my life played out as a child, I should have emerged from childhood seriously damaged. It is a constant reminder of God's hand of mercy and grace over me. Not to say I wasn't hurt and wounded to such a degree that it has cost me dearly over the course of my life, however it pales in comparison to what it could have been.

When I look back and relive how overly strict my mom was from my perspective, I wonder if she was under the impression that her silence about such dangers protected me. If she only knew that my life was consumed with fear of the unknowns. If she only knew how those real fears played out in my life on a personal level. I have come to see over the years that she was protecting me. However, I don't believe she ever looked at the bigger picture.

Communication wasn't a normal practice between kids and adults of long ago. I just wanted her to know that she could trust me. Why didn't she just share with me those dangers in my neighborhood that she was aware of so that I would not have misinterpreted her behavior. I was far too afraid of her to disobey her, and the real likelihood of her dying prevented me from doing anything that would potentially hurt her to any appreciable degree. Everyone has their own way of showing love, and over the years of me reliving parts of my childhood, I came to see her definition of love.

Our living room was converted to a bedroom/sitting room with my mom's hospital bed taking up much of the room. Our bedrooms were upstairs. I worried that someone would break into our apartment and hurt my mom. I always seemed to be so far from her at night. I felt helpless. I would lie on my bed and stare at the window in my bedroom. There were always noises that seemed to indicate trouble. The government had given my mom a window-unit air conditioner because she had a lung removed due to cancer. There was a gap between the air conditioner and the window which made me think how easy it would be for someone to break in.

My mom needed the air conditioner. She struggled at times to breathe. I worried myself sick because she only had one lung. She continued to smoke. I would never come to terms with that. I was so afraid that she would die when she had a coughing attack. She couldn't catch her breath at times. One day the ambulance was called, and I thought this was it. I am going to be without a mom. She would recover time and time again. When would her next coughing attack be her last?

Fear seemed to represent everything in my life. I never had the opportunity to let my guard down, or so it seemed. Things were always happening that increased my fear. I heard a loud noise in our kitchen only to discover that someone had shot another BB through our kitchen window. I'm not sure if this was intentional. Our back yard slopped down to our elementary school. My mind would immediately go to the worst scenario. Perhaps someone was randomly shooting. The bullets lodged into the window pane. My mom had to check it out. She scared me to death. I wonder if I would have had a meltdown now and again, would that have potentially awakened her to my fears. I would catch her eyes looking at me, but she never said a word, she was completely silent. She never questioned my silence. Didn't my eyes show my fear. I waited for her to say something again and again. I was ready to listen and to give her feedback as I see it now.

One night, A stranger was banging on random doors who was apparently drunk asking the neighbors for money. After ignoring him for a time, my mom told him that she was sick and didn't have any money. This left me with yet another layer of fear. I am surprised at times that I didn't literally die of fright in those days. You can't argue with the obvious!

I was under the impression that I could be quiet, stay hidden and avoid all groups of people, only to discover those piercing stares by some that seemed to literally cripple me every morning and afternoon when I rode the bus to high school. The bus was always full of people, so when the students got on, most had to stand up. Standing up blocked the view of those sitting down. Being glared at for 45 minutes by those who chose staring as a sport didn't help a little white girl who was scared of her own shadow.

When I start to put these experiences down on paper, I am forced to see those innumerable times when God unbeknownst to me, had miraculously intervened in my life.

God's Sovereignty plays out every single time in a true believer's life. Nothing and no one can thwart God's Sovereignty in our lives. The problem for me was that I couldn't imagine that my life growing up in poverty was ok with the God of the Universe. How could God allow me to be without a father, and have a sick mom who couldn't meet my needs? Living in poverty on this level and not having a way out says it all. I couldn't conceive of the idea that my life in poverty was God's Sovereign Will for my life. These two opposing things sure didn't add up to God's love for me. No one else according to my knowledge had to live this life that I was forced to call my reality.

All other young believers had the material things vital to life. They also had a mom and a dad in their homes. They had grandparents and other family members who played instrumental roles in their lives. I felt cheated by God himself. How can that be. He loves everyone unconditionally. His word says that he blesses his children. Was I the exception to the "rule"? I seemed to live this "rule" out personally. It never got easier and my life never matched up with others. From my perspective, I was never included in anything good, and the facts always seemed to line up to support my perspective.

As I continued to go to church. I would come to my own conclusion the life we live was the result of my mom not being a Christian. Other kids in my church had moms who came to church with them, and their lives were much better. My mom did set the stage for how we were to conduct ourselves at church and at school. She did her part as a parent teaching her kids behind the scenes. She didn't have to be with us to assure our obedience to others. Back then children knew their places. Her expectation of obedience was on a different level as I reminiscence of long ago.

Unbeknownst to her, she failed in giving me the needed permission to stand up for myself as a child. I was fully aware that if I would have found myself in trouble at school, I would be the guilty one. She never tolerated disobedience on any level. I never got into any "real" trouble at school. However, when you are guilty before proven innocence, you live with the fear that you are going to pay someone else's consequences sooner or later. My mom wasn't aware that she left me incredibly vulnerable.

I had to be on the outside looking in to make sense of it all. She wanted others to see that although she had to endure what bad health and poverty would bring her, she wanted people to see that her children were taught to be upstanding and responsible people. Respect for adults had a different meaning 50 years ago than it does today. I knew that I would suffer the consequence if I disrespected any adult. I can't allow myself to call older people by their first names to this day.

I would find myself living out a different kind of consequence as a result of my desperate need to have things that other kids in my neighborhood were accustomed to having. The same food truck that would frequent our neighborhood in the summer months happened to be parked on my street and a friend bought something and told the owner to put her purchase on her mom's tab. The owner would ask me what I wanted, so I decided to get a piece of candy and to ask him to put it on my mom's tab. I felt empowered and convicted at the same time. Although the owner was fine with granting my request, he later told my mom. Needless to say, my mom made me go right back to apologize. That was one of the few times I got spanked.

My mom had scruples and morals and I appreciated this. She obeyed those in authority and taught us to do the same, and I equally grew to appreciate this. However, putting herself in an inferior position to everyone she met didn't serve me well. She never seemed to be envious of what others had. She was fine with what others in our neighborhood gained along the way. My mom never had an opinion one way or another.

Did her dreaded life cause her to forget what it was like when she was child? Did she grow up as the underdog? Because I had become accustomed to always being left out in my church, at my school, and witnessing the neighborhood kids always having gum, candy, and soda; I wanted some as well. I was a kid. I see now that I coveted their candy daily.

The only time I heard the word "coveted" was at Church. I must have missed the meaning of the word. Or perhaps my flesh superseded, and I simply ignored it. Teasing was a word in my vocabulary that I was forced to attach to myself as a child. I was ready for a new word to add to my vocabulary. How about "Mercy" from this man who told my mom about a small piece of candy. The candy that I "bought" from the candy truck probably cost five cents. This would be a red flag, as I see now. I was a young child. One piece of candy put on a tab. The word *dumb* comes to mind. If I were smarter, I would have gotten more than one piece. I got a spanking for lying, the amount of candy was not the issue.

My mom was terrific with her modest funds. She only purchased the basics. She didn't need to make a grocery list, that's for sure. Although I couldn't put it into words, I felt at times that something just didn't seem right, when she would share with our neighbors a needed cup of sugar or a cup of flour and I was never permitted to purchase a piece or two of candy from the food truck as my neighbors did. I can't imagine ignoring a kid who is left out amongst their peers. These kids apparently didn't know the word "share". They should have, after all my mom shared with their mom's. I never asked them to share. I never ask anyone for anything. I haven't quite figured that one out.

The neighbors knew of my moms' bad health, but they never offered a helping hand. Perhaps the reason they dealt kindly with her was because they could depend on her at times. Life was much different for me. I guess being a child didn't afford me the kindness from most in my neighborhood. Being secluded from the majority of our neighborhood didn't allow us to meet other kids. Perhaps they thought we didn't like them. My mom just kept us in close proximity to her. Even when she slept the day away, we knew the perimeters.

Month after month my mom was given food stamps, and she would bring home the same ole huge five-pound log of cheese, the same ole huge solid log of disgusting bologna, large quantities of eggs, a huge bag of sugar, and a huge bag of flour. I didn't like thick bologna or cheese; so needless to say, those foods did nothing for me. As I look back, I never saw her excited or joyful about the food either. Another example of simply surviving. Perhaps, she didn't feel good about being in the position that required our family to depend on the government. I, on the other hand never felt good about anything in my life.

Although my mom never shared her hurts with me at this point in her life, I learned from her consistent behavior that she had her own share of hurts and pain. She had her own childhood secrets. Her mom came to help her when she had lung surgery. Out of the blue her mom simply stopped coming. I was around 8 years of age. She lived an hour or so away. I would not get to know her as my grandmother, or have a relationship with her. I would learn that my grandmother lived to be in her 80's. Not having any extended family was just another example of what defined my personal consistency. I would be forced to attach the meaning of "alone", "rejected" and "ostracized" to me personally as I grew up.

I would find myself looking at my mom's facial expressions at times when she was either speaking to her physician on the phone, or when she would reach out to her family with little response. Her many voids would add up to mere survival. Her expectations were dangerously low. Children being like sponges, I absorbed that same fatalism into my own way of thinking which led me to emulate her hopelessness, resulting in despair. If she would have had any fight in her at all, I would have emulated that and perhaps changed the direction of my life. My mom would sleep most days, especially in the summer months. She would sit out on the stoop late at night smoking. Her only lung was diseased with emphysema. Just another piece of my life that I couldn't comprehend.

I wondered what kept her up at night just staring into space and puffing on her cigarettes. Her loneliness, and hopelessness silently screamed her reality. I couldn't sleep until she came in, closed the door and locked its many locks. She never spoke a single word of her disappointments in life. However, her mood screamed how overwhelmed she was. Her only vices were smoking and Pepsi. Two things she never shared.

Although my mom was sick all the time, her six children were rarely sick. We had nearly perfect attendance every year while in elementary school. I'm sure school was a break for my mom, giving her a measure of needed and well-deserved peace that helped to save her sanity against all odds. I began to accept things for how they were, even though at times, many times I would come to my wits' end and sob my eyes out.

My personal life was so bad that I began to stop questioning anything. I stopped attaching myself to anything I couldn't achieve. This was my method of self-protection. It simply wasn't in the cards for me. The disappointments were just too consistent, and the constant pain was unbearable at times.

My fellow students who had the world in the palms of their hands as they came to believe; I have wondered at times where they are today. They had everything from my perspective, good and bad. Did their parties, drugs, money and total freedom along with all their desires granted to them serve them well. Are their lives productive today?

Are they living the dream as they were made to believe they would? Did such behavior, and their many choices of which were short-lived negatively affect some of them to the degree that it crippled them for life? Did some regret identifying with a world that included drugs that had the real likelihood of leading them down a road of no return? Not to stereotype, but facts support this thought. Did their behavior result in a life of crime? Did the alcohol, drugs and inappropriate behavior cost some of them their very lives along the way?

If I close my eyes and see the behavior of those kids who were bused to my school along with the kids from my neighborhood, I see a lot of obvious differences, including the different shades of skin, and different backgrounds that can discriminate. Equally I see many similarities, drugs, alcohol and inappropriate behavior of which don't discriminate.

The path that I had to walk caused me to be helpless and hopeless in all areas of my life. I was a victim ready to be used and abused in many horrible ways. All the hurts and rejections I experienced paralyzed me on most levels. My hope at the end of the day is whom I belong to. My fellow students would not have changed places with me for a mere second. They had it all from their perspective. I didn't want their drugs and behavior, however, I longed to have their material things, and their freedom to name a few. Would they have changed their minds knowing what they know now? Would they have joined me in my life knowing the end result? I could not have imagined that I would be able to say with confidence nearly a life time later that I was exceedingly blessed above those I wanted to emulate, because of who I was in Christ Jesus long ago.

I am resolved to put my childhood behind me with Gods' help. I am resolved to embrace my position in the Lord. I am resolved to do whatever I can to bring glory to Gods' name. I am resolved to trust God with me, not just in mere words, but in actions as well.

When you come to some level of maturity, realizing this life on earth is a mere blink of an eye compared to eternity in heaven, it helps to put it into perspective. Reminiscing about those students who had the things that I so desperately wanted long ago shows me how much my personal consistency's hurt me to the core and crippled me emotionally. I wonder what did their own personal consistency's cost them?

As I relive the behaviors of the students of long ago that I envied causes my heart to skip a beat all these years later. I think of those who thought they had everything that completed them. Those who were misguided by their peers. The unhealthy freedom given by parents potentially lead them down a path some now regret. Are these students equally independent of God in their lives?

Not having your crucial needs met that cripple you from functioning in society has a silver lining when compared to being crippled as the result of a life of drugs, alcohol and devoid of God himself. Every human being has a void within themselves that we spend our lives trying to fill. The truth is there is a God-shaped void in our heart that can only be filled by him.

When we want to depend on others for our worth, we become focused on earthly things that never satisfy. When we mimic others to gain approval, we are left incredibly disappointed. The world in large wants instant gratification so much of the time. We want our little world to validate us. We depend on our own strength to gain that which we desire. This will all lead to emptiness. As believers this mindset causes us to lose sweet fellowship with the Lord. As unbelievers this mindset causes one to be separated from the God of the Universe for all eternity.

Growing up in poverty almost prevented me from functioning in society as a whole person. It didn't for one reason and one reason alone, because I belonged to God and he prevented me from being a statistic.

God permitted me to live the way I did. He allowed me to feel hopeless. He allowed me to be unprepared, ill equipped, and voided as a child. He was right beside me every step of the way. I would finally come to this realization years later that the footprints in the sand are personal to me.

My God is now using all that my life entailed, to grow me, teach me, and to guide me. He is preparing me for his Kingdom. I was not created for this Earthly Kingdom. It is not designed to last. It is not my home; I am simply passing through. Only what I do for Christ Jesus while on this earth will last.

When I think of my mom, I think of the story of the two sinners on the cross with Jesus. Neither had lived a life for God. One came to believe while he hung on the cross, and Jesus promised that he would be with him in paradise, while the other chose his fate apart from God. My mom came to know Jesus as her personal Lord and Savior later in life. She didn't display what Jesus meant to her as I was blessed to do. She didn't witness to others the good news of Jesus Christ as I have had the pleasure of doing. She didn't raise her kids for the glory of God as I lived to do with Gods leading. Her life on earth didn't afford her time to grow in the Lord as it has allowed me.

I fall to my knees when I think of Gods' grace and mercy that he offers to all who would heed his voice when he calls. My mom heeded Gods' call and accepted him as her own personal Lord and Savior. I don't know how I would have emotionally handled life all these years since my mom died, if I did not know for sure that she is safe in the arms of Jesus.

I have wanted to believe that God's grace and mercy covered my mom because she exercised her own free Will to allow her kids to go to church. She had no clue as to what kind of church it was. However, God protected her and ultimately protected her children. Did my mom ever see how Gods' hand of protection was over her and her children.

I wonder if I would have had my needs met when I was young, and if I had those momentary things that others enjoyed; would I have trusted all of me with the one true God of the Universe. Could I have potentially lost out on what I did receive, eternity with Christ Jesus.

A momentary feel-good, a momentary taste-good, a momentary rise in self-esteem that the world promises, is just that; momentary. God promises eternity to all those who belong to him. All sin will be wiped away. No more hurt or pain of any kind, no more division, no more teasing, no more heartache, and no more fear that grips you, controls you, and cripples you. I couldn't see past the pain that left me feeling hopeless.

When I was a young person, a teenager, or even a young adult, I didn't have the tools to make sense of anything; those needed tools to put anything into its right perspective. We are judged by God for what we know, not for what we don't know. To whom he gives much, God expects much. God says it and that settles it! I see vividly how I walked around so numb and so invisible. It would take years for me to see in spite of how I had to grow up, God protected me when I was so lost. There simply is no other explanation.

The experience of having my hair nearly burned, chased by bullies, constantly being made fun of, and tolerating the harsh words that was hurled at me daily kept me paralyzed. This blinded me to Gods' presence in my life. I feel ashamed that I allowed those who bullied me to have such a hold on me. I would shake in my boots with my knees buckling and my heart pounding, not knowing if I was going to live or die. I read the verse that says God will right all wrongs when he returns to judge the world. Was he speaking to me personally? I wasn't given the needed permission to protect myself, or stand up for myself. I wasn't given the self-esteem needed to stop the bullies in their tracks. I find it interesting that although my little world didn't see me or value me, the bullies seemed to always find me, and use my insecurities against me.

Not being aware of anyone protecting me throughout my life could be the reason as to why I own verses that speak loud and clear of Gods' protection over his own. It was my only hope in a world that didn't see me. My God said no to anything worse happening to me that would have profoundly affected me. Having the confidence that he can take any heartache or any horrific thing and turn it around, and use it for his ultimate glory would take on a different meaning as I continued to grow in his word.

I feel that God took my mom home at a time when her physical body simply could not keep up with the needed demands. God spared her more of the endless hurt and pain that she would have had to endure if she lived. I still struggle trying to comprehend my mom's life and the many health problems that plagued her. I didn't have the tools back then to really empathize with her pain. My peace comes from knowing that she will never ever suffer again. God heard my cry when I ask him to take me before he takes my mom. He heard my desperate plea to not separate me from my mom. He answered my prayer according to his sovereignty as he always does.

CHAPTER 9

THE LIGHT IS REVEALED

Job 12:22

I would lie in my bed night after night having no words to truly explain why my life was so saturated with fear. This was one of the reasons I floundered as a child, and it would be one of the reasons that I floundered on some levels as an adult. This has taken me nearly a lifetime to come to terms with. I recognized at times while in the depths of despair, I would plead with God to take away the fear that kept me from having an ounce of hope that was potentially out there for me, of which I couldn't see. My circumstances were such that I allowed them to overshadow, control, rule and ultimately paralyze me. Although I did choose to believe that God loved me, I allowed society, the secular world and the Christian world to define me, place me in a box and dictate to me on all levels. Somehow the emotional voids that led to my emotional paralysis wouldn't allow me to see the bigger picture until I grew up.

In my God given desire to learn more about the one true God to whom I belonged to; I would begin reading more of my bible, praying that he would reveal himself to me in a way only he could. I started on my journey which has taken me to where I am now, with years in between. The more I earnestly prayed in desperation for God's truth to flood over me; for his presence to illuminate me, for his unconditional love to saturate me, and for his healing hand to heal me on all levels; I would begin to see glimpses of him, which over time would shape me, so as to see him mightily in my life, even at times when fear seemed to supersede.

The process I describe here seemingly took a lifetime. I would find myself taking two steps forward, four steps back, five steps forward, six steps back, eight steps forward, six steps back, four steps forward, three steps back, and before I knew it, an occasional step back. This would begin to prove to me that God was directing my steps. I would earnestly pray for God to nearly drown me with wisdom, so as to not find myself regressing in my walk with him.

As I began to draw close to him, his promise to draw close to me was becoming evident in my life. Fear that once gripped me, controlled me, and nearly owned me was beginning to have a different meaning to me, something that has profoundly changed me and continues to change me from the inside out.

Proverbs 9:10 says, "The fear of the Lord is the beginning of wisdom, and the knowledge of the Holy One is understanding" KJV. The fear of God is foundational to true wisdom; all other types of learning are worthless unless built upon the knowledge of the Lord himself. In the Bible the word translated as "fear" refers to the terror one feels in a frightening situation, as I experienced over the course of my life. It can also mean "respect" in the sense of a person honoring those in authority. Fear can also denote the reverence and *awe* a person feels in the presence of greatness. I equally experienced this as I grew in my faith.

In order to develop the fear of the Lord, we must recognize God for who he is. We must have a mere glimpse with our spirits of the power, might, beauty, and brilliance of God almighty. Those who fear the Lord have a continual awareness of him, a profound deep reverence for him, and a sincere commitment to obey him in all our actions, words, and deeds to the best of our ability, recognizing that we can do nothing without the hand of God directing us in every area of our lives. This is a guarantee that we can do all things through Christ who strengthens us. Fear had a polar opposite meaning for me as an innocent child growing up in poverty.

I realized something years later that if I gained the needed tools growing up, perhaps I would have not questioned God, and at times choosing to blame him for my many deficits. I was constantly forced to see all that was available to everyone in my world, but that world excluded me on every level possible.

If I never had gone to Bible Camp, I could have relinquished the temptations and the teasing. If I never had gone to church, I would have been spared the reality that even a Christian's vital needs are met. If I had never met those kids who were bused to my school, I would have been spared the disappointments that came as a result of being born on the wrong side of the tracks. When God delivered me of much, these disappointments would be short lived as I looked at the bigger picture many years later. However, it didn't help when I was forced to live it day in and day out.

The kids in my church were afforded so much more than I was afforded, and although I was blessed to be picked up for church week after week, I was still forced to see the injustices from a child's point of view. Discovering that true believer's vital needs were seemingly met on all levels was just another message that screamed loud and clear to me that I absolutely did not matter.

Having the needed self-esteem, which I would later equate to being loved unconditionally was something I coveted. Having skills that would allow me to fit in and feel "normal" was something I desired. After all, everyone else in my own little world seemed to be "normal". This would have been the difference of me always finding myself alone and rejected, to finding myself joining in; having some of the same experiences and fond memories that others had. These experiences simply made life easier, something that I had no chance of gaining, bar none!

I would learn along my journey what God expects of his children, to be *in* this world, not be *of* this world's philosophy. I learned that this knowledge was crucial to a true believer. When I was a child, I didn't want the world's philosophy. I didn't even comprehend that word. I wanted my crucial needs met. I can say with a clear conscience that I NEEDED my crucial needs met.

My extreme poverty may have caused me to want what the Christian world had, but in all fairness, I was a child. Years later, my God would begin to reveal to me exactly what it all meant. One major reality equal to my own reality as a young person living in poverty, was that we live in a fallen world with fallen people just like me. I finally shared something with the rest of society. Once again, bittersweet.

"Jesus replied: Love the Lord your God with all your heart, and with all your soul and with all thy mind". Matthew 22:37 NIV

God expects us to conform to the image of his Son. I heard it all before in my head as a child growing up in poverty. I would begin to hear it with my heart.

I was deeply moved when I read what God says in Romans 12:1-2 NASB "I urge you therefore brethren, by the mercies of God to present your bodies a living sacrifice, holy acceptable unto God which is your spiritual service. And do not be conformed to this world, but be transformed by the renewing of your mind that you may prove what the will of God is, that which is good and acceptable and perfect will of God." Giving all of me to God and him alone would begin to saturate my mind. Slowly letting go of the flesh would be liberating.

I would begin to comprehend the meaning of verses as I studied Gods' word. After true salvation the believer lives a life under Gods' influence. Yielding to the Spirit as he leads, and allowing the Holy Spirit to transform and renew the mind daily of every believer is key in our spiritual walk. The mind of Christ involves wisdom from God, once hidden but now revealed to true believers. God would reveal these truths to me along my life's journey. My problem was that I was impatient waiting for Gods' wisdom that would guide and direct my steps. I still had one foot pointing down and one foot pointing up. I was divided. I just didn't fully know it. Reliving my past of endless voids haunted me.

My emotions absolutely controlled me. Although emotions are wonderful things; after all, God created them, but unless they are shaped by a mind saturated in God's truth, they can be destructive, out-of-control forces. This I know. Where the mind goes, the *will* follows, and so do the emotions. My emotions were all over the place trying to wrap my head around a society in which I was born in, created by God himself and like everyone else, but so ill equipped.

Years and years later I would find that growing in the word of God was gaining me an insatiable appetite for the word of God, when I put him first in my life. This knowledge would be life changing for me. As I would make a choice to be obedient to God, he would prove himself to me as he promises. Verses that I had read over and over began jumping off the pages at times. I am humble in how God was opening my eyes and ears to his truth.

As a young child going to Church, I believed what my teachers taught me; never questioning or having an opinion. I simply obeyed. Whatever they would have told me, I would not have questioned; this I am confident of. God in his goodness prevented me from hearing a false gospel as a child. This insight began to reveal to me that although the world failed me on every single level, my God did not. He just didn't stop all that I had to go through as a child growing up in poverty.

However, I received Gods' truth, the only truth that can save a soul; this very truth that saved my soul. Unfortunately, there are churches on every corner that are devoid of Gods' truth. They are leading so many down a path that can only lead to Hell. Gods' truth has always stood up, and will always stand up against any false teaching because false teaching contradicts his word.

To accept anything less than 100% of God's truth is to be eventually led down a road spiritually speaking, that could cause one to buy into a philosophy that they would have never dreamt they would buy into. Visiting other churches as an adult began to worry me at times that I may be listening to the wrong message from those who preached Gods' word. When you are cheated out of vital tools needed in life, and people treat you as a second-class citizen, you don't have the healthy self-esteem that will grant you confidence at times when you need it most. When you are taught to obey adults to an absolute fault, it can potentially set you up to believe lies from those who are not led by God.

Finding myself depending on a fallen world that will always fail you didn't allow me to separate the church from the world. I classified "believers" as I did society in large. Based on what they had, where they lived, and who their families were forced me to accept that everyone was superior to me. I came to the conclusion that I would never be able to relate to my world. This would cause me to worry so much that it drained my energy and kept me in a fog.

I would learn later in life that my understanding of the words *fear* and *worry* wasn't categorically wrong; it's just that the admonishment against fear and worry wasn't applicable or relevant to me. I allowed my position, and my voids based on my dire and unfortunate circumstances to dictate my worth. This became a habit that followed me into adulthood that left me hopeless and helpless.

Allowing others to form my opinion of who I was according to their standards never served me well, as I look back with tears flowing down my cheeks. I imagine how much better, not perfect, mind you, and not like most, some areas of my life could have been, if I had allowed God to define my self-worth. It could have changed the direction of my life, or at least could have spared me a measure of unnecessary pain that I lived in day after day, and year after year, only to find myself all grown up, regardless if I was emotionally ready.

CHAPTER 10

ALL GROWN UP

Colossians 2:7

Immediately upon graduation, I began to serve as a nanny for a family from church. I loved those kids. I now see them in a different light with families of their own. We had a blast during those years. I would look after them five days a week and often take them home with me on weekends. We went to parks together and did things such as walking, biking, throwing stones in the lake, reading, going on outings, preparing meals, and watching movies. I have wonderful memories.

There came a time when I desperately needed to supplement my income. I was hired to work at McDonald's for a few hours each week. After some time, I was offered a manager's position. I never thought that I would be chosen to be a manager anywhere. It was out of my league, or so I thought. The increase in pay made my choice a no-brainer. I desperately needed the money. My six-day work week didn't allow me to continue to look after the kids that I fell in love with. I would still entertain them when I could.

My years working at McDonald's as a manager served me well. With much enthusiasm, I enjoyed the challenges and took pride in my store. Cleanliness all the way! I was primarily the day manager.

One day, the night manager asked if I would take her shift that evening. She had an unexpected exam the next day. The supervisor gave me permission. I went home to get some rest before I came back for the evening shift.

Everything was going smoothly until a customer came up to tell me that his sandwich wasn't well done. I proceeded to ask one of my crew members to make him another sandwich. It was time to close and I locked the door preventing anyone from coming into the store, allowing the last customer to leave at his convenience. This would be my mistake. I began taking the cash drawers to my desk in the back of the restaurant to count the money as was customary.

The customer came back up and pointed a gun at me, sticking it in my gut. There were four crew members remaining on the shift. I told them just to stand still. The guy proceeded to guide me to the back of the restaurant with his gun now sticking into my back. He jerked the phone out of the wall. He was not the least bit nervous, so I followed his instructions to a T. He took the money and then locked us in a "two-way lock" freezer ordering us to stay for half an hour or else he would kill us. We stayed longer.

When we finally emerged, we went down the street to the fire station and called the police. That was a scary experience for all of us. When I recall the fear of the unknown that plagued me as a child, and I compare it with this fear resulting from a new experience, it puts it into perspective. However, fear is fear, and personally I have had my full share.

Two or three days later, I awoke in the middle of the night sobbing after reliving this experience in a dream. Managers were responsible for their crew, and I must have suppressed my emotions and processed it in my sleep. It would take time for the fear to totally leave me. Having to go to the Police Station to look through mugshots kept the memory from fading. They never found this person which saved me from more fear in having to identify him.

I took such pride in being a manager. Our ultimate job was to keep the customers returning (not the ones carrying guns). I took pride in training my crew to be their best. Teaching them how to prepare food that was not only tasty, but pleasing to the eye for all to see; apparently a new concept for some based on how they cooked. We had QSC (quality, service and cleanliness) competitions with other stores and we won most of them. I loved the accolades, and I needed approval for a job well done.

This job was needed for the obvious. It served me well for four plus years. My husband and I would soon be blessed with a family. I decided to be a stay-at-home mom. I began to supplement my income by babysitting other children. This ended up working out well. I was elated to be a mom and wanted to pour my heart and life into my kids. Working outside the home was not an option for me.

Managing a restaurant required me to work six days a week, coupled with evening meetings didn't justify me working. I chose to babysit and clean houses and offices to make ends meet. I thank God to this day that I was not forced to work outside the home. God doesn't give us any more than we can handle. This would be the beginning of my personal testimony of how God has continued to care for me in such personal ways all these years later.

I wrote a poem to express my thoughts and feelings of long ago.

> Many times, I have wondered where I've been…
> Who I am, and if I fit in…
> Making believe kept me alone…
> In my own little world, where I was emotionally on my own…
> Patiently waiting for anyone to notice, although to me unknown…
> There is a hope that others seem to have, which was in them sown…
> And I'm left to figure it out, wanting to belong…
> While pondering when it will end, those many times keeping my head in a spin…
> Circumstances that would never allow me to have the dream to win…
> Only to learn through all my countless fears…
> Continually producing an unexpected flood of tears…
> I may not by the world's standards ever belong…
> Or have within me my own personal victory song…
> But I now see with confidence that which society threw at me…
> My God took it all using it per his Sovereignty…
> To grow me in who he is calling me to be…

My ignorance allowed me to blame God for the circumstances in my life. Envying what others had in their lives, their families, their way of living, their status, their material things and their self-esteem equated to unconditional love from my perspective. I really had nothing to compare this too. However, I wanted to experience it personally. I measured their worth by their families, their countless things, their outings and how happy they appeared.

Becoming an adult doesn't erase the past whether the memories are fond, or not so fond. Although, I envied those things necessary to life that others had. I never really envied them their food, and I would be so hungry at times at school. I wondered how my brain even functioned. I did struggle at times in high school. My problem was obviously a prolonged lack of nutrition judging from the discoveries I made when I did eat.

The school programs of today have come a long way in how they operate to protect kids who are from low-income families. I understand now that my refusal to eat was related to pride. I was a child with voids on top of voids. Some handle such a situation better than I obviously did. My reality may not be yours, and your reality may not be mine. To judge another before you exchange places with them will keep one blind from the needs of others.

My "reality" of being born in poverty is equal to the "reality" of me being born again bought by the precious blood of Jesus Christ. The stark difference is a life lived apart from Christ Jesus is separation from God for all eternity. The end result of a life of poverty for a true born-again believer is reigning with Jesus Christ for all eternity. The key word here is "Jesus Christ" and in him alone.

Although I am unequivocally the epitome of a weak and voided person by the world's standards, I am indwelled with the Holy Spirit and because of him, I am continuously made strong. I am never alone, or ever on my own.

What I struggled with most of my young life was not having the needed tools that were necessary in every aspect of your lives. I was fully aware that we live in a fallen world because of Adam and Eve's sin. However, not being prepared for society will leave you with insurmountable wounds that never seem to heal.

Before a baby is able to eat solid foods, he or she has to grow teeth. Before a child can read, he or she must learn the alphabet. Before one can graduate to the next stage of development, they must complete the stage of development they are currently in. A student doesn't comprehend high school courses until they comprehend middle school courses, unless they are one of those extraordinary exceptions to the rule.

My pain as immense and inexplicable as it was, caused me to question God at times, instead of trusting him with me. When my circumstances never changed for the better, I couldn't pray. I didn't feel worthy. Society did such a number on me psychologically that I couldn't even think for myself. When I find myself attempting to make sense of my life, I find myself reliving the same questions I did as a child growing up in poverty. These same questions that I simply had no answers for turned into decades.

I would be reminded of how short this life on earth is. What I have supersedes anything this earth has to offer. Being truly born again does not eradicate the pain in one's life. Having the Holy Spirit inside with the confidence that God is walking right beside you doesn't erase all the sad memories of long ago. Coming to a point in your life that you no longer depend on this world to sustain you, by allowing God to finally complete you, is when you begin to see the bigger picture.

I have grown the most in my walk with the Lord during the really tough times. This is not to say that I didn't want to throw in the spiritual towel. Thanks to God, I didn't succumb to that temptation. There were so many times when God didn't appear to be enough for me. If he were enough, why did I see death as the only way out? I used to wonder where God was during those time's I felt so low. Why would my Lord and Savior allow me to go so low, and stay there for so long? Did God allow me to be rejected by the world, to save me from the world?

Once I grasped the reality that the pain of all my voids, my circumstances, my heartache, my emptiness, and my rejection by others did not define me, I began to realize that Jesus Christ suffered so much more for me, and therefore he understood what I was going through. And because he knows what is best for me, he allowed me to endure it. It has taken me years to see that I wasn't alone. Why did I feel alone too many times to count when I was too young to comprehend?

"These things I have spoken to you, that in me you may have peace. In this world you will have tribulation, but be of good cheer, I have overcome the world." John 16:33 NKJV A hard and impossible verse for an innocent and naive child to comprehend. I wondered if this verse and others like it only applied to adults. I couldn't possibly grasp it as a child.

A child who grows up in extreme poverty, devoid of every single tool that is critical in moving forward in every stage of development is one thing. To find yourself in the adult world that has its own set of rules and expectations is even worse. If you fall behind in every stage of development as a child, isn't it a given that those same voids you lived out as a child will most certainly follow you into adulthood, impacting you on a much larger scale.

Poverty should not equate to unkindness by others. It should not equate to being ignored and ostracized by those who feel superior. Poverty should not equate to unfairness because you can't relate. It should not take away every ounce of hope that others around you are blessed to have. It shouldn't equate to having your heart ripped out of your chest time and time again.

On one hand, all true believer's live in a fallen world. On the other, there is no excuse. On one hand, all true believer's sin because they are sinners. On the other, there is no excuse. On one hand, the Holy Spirit takes up residence in all true believers the moment of conversion. On the other, this security doesn't give believers a license to sin habitually.

I read that "Our heart can't seem to delete, so we must be intentional and learn to turn off the negative thoughts that could derail us back to our past. We must take ownership of our past experiences and recognize our old habits and old patterns of doing things. I can live my life moving forward, but only understanding it backwards". When I look back even when it brings tears, has shown me clearly where God has taken me from and where he is leading me now. When we have a growth mindset, our setbacks become less detrimental because we have acquired new knowledge and find ourselves better equipped to learn and grow through the adversities.

If we are never given the needed permission to grieve or vent our frustrations, we have a hard time recovering emotionally. If we never feel safe, we become vulnerable.

"The Lord is near to the brokenhearted and saves the crushed in spirit" Psalm 34:18 NIV I had to own this verse and apply it to me personal. Even when I find myself so alone and rejected at times, I know that he is watching over me, not because I feel it, but because the word of God says it. My trust, hope, and my faith is in the Lord. "What can mere man do to me?" I simply had to obey this truth.

These facts and truths about my life didn't prevent me from caring for others. It didn't cause me to hate the human race. It didn't prevent me from having a heart for the young and old alike. Working with children gave me the desire to be a mom for as long as I can remember. Caring for children seemed to fill a void in me. I am still thanking God for blessing me to be a mom. I poured into my kids everything that wasn't poured into me. They were served meals that put smiles on their faces. They had choices. They had voices. They were listened too, and they were spoken too. Everything that wasn't afforded to me, I would give to my kids. I worked endlessly to prevent voids in my kids' lives. I did it out of love. I couldn't bear to see them walk in my shoes. It would have emotionally destroyed me.

How can someone who is born into a world devoid of the vital tools and lacking in the necessary skills actually make it. How do you make something out of nothing? How do you bounce back from being a shell of a person? How do you pull up your bootstraps and make it, when you don't even have boots? I liken it to a having a defibrillator, an apparatus used to control heart fibrillation by application of an electric current to the chest wall or heart. Who is in control here? How are you staying alive? How much control do you really have?

I used to ask, "Where are you God?" I mean, he could have stepped in. He could have stopped the madness. At what point does someone suffer more as the result of who their parents are; the families in which they are born into, and the choices they make. Parents consequences will negatively affect their children on countless levels. Some consequences are "short lived", others give new meaning to "long lived". In my case, "seemingly forever". "Forever" is all relative.

I can't remember ever holding it against my mom how I had to live when I was a child. However, I had to call it what it was for my own healing. She was a product of her environment, as I was a product of mine. She had been sick as a child and her health got worse, with so many health problems that it not only seemed unreal, it screamed, "Unfair!" This knowledge helped me to put it into perspective on some level. In saying that, no amount of knowledge that I gained about my life, or how much I put it into its rightful perspective to the smallest degree, will ever change or undo how my life played out. You just move forward and wake up one day wondering how you got from where you started and where you are now.

The numbness that was a part of my DNA as a child would be equal to my life as a young adult. I would find myself still forced to taste the unkindness, rejection, and cruelty by others. No longer was I able to ignore it, assume it was normal, or simply overlook it as I did most of my life. Being a target as a result of having low expectations can play out by others who define you. My low expectations which gave new meaning to the word *low*, continued to teach me much.

I would listen to Dr. Paul Meier speak on his book "Don't let the Jerks get the better of you" He would talk about setting boundaries with those who see you as weak. Unfortunately, this would prove itself over and over again just how much we live in a fallen depraved world. Drawing boundaries didn't gain me acceptance either. If you are deemed second class, setting boundaries isn't going to gain you entrance. Speaking up for myself created its own heartaches. Stepping back only left me feeling more alone. Some of the same pain and heartache as an adult would take me back to my childhood of long ago. Seemingly like a lateral move, just older.

The silver lining would come when I realized that I had a voice for those who walked in my shoes. Because I lived it, I could offer support to others who were marginalized by society. They needed to know that they were equally created in Gods' image. Something I had a hard time owning myself, as a result of how society used my impoverished life against me.

Choosing to depend on God to define me would be superseded by mankind. I thought society had what I needed based on what I observed. I guess it was instant gratification I craved. I frantically wanted to escape my past at all cost, never to return. I desperately wanted to forget, start over and never be reminded how horrific my life as child had been. I wanted my story to die along with me so that no one on this earth would ever know. The fact that I couldn't totally escape it was because God is in control, not me. Obedience to my Lord and Savior slowly began to give me insight into what God had in store for me according to his Sovereignty and his perfect timing, not mine.

God would begin to guide me, and use me in places that would grow me in ways that only he could deem possible. If I could have seen the future from a child's point of view, my flesh would have refused to go. God knows what we need to know, and the time frame in which we need to know it.

One place where God would use me years and years later would be working with the homeless. Churches who participated in this ministry would open up their doors during the cold months to give homeless men a hot meal and a warm bed each night. These men had their clothes laundered. They had choices of attending a Bible study, watching a sports game on television, and enjoying fellowship with the volunteers. Each day they were served a warm breakfast and were given a packed lunch to take with them back to the streets, where unfortunately they lived. There would be many reasons why they were homeless.

We called them our guests. We loved on them, shared the good news of Jesus Christ with them, listened to their hearts, and prayed with them. We continue to pray for them. Many would come back weekly for years. There were those who got jobs, slowly re-entering society as productive citizens. I would tell them that it was by the grace of God that those of us who were volunteers were not homeless, conveying to them that they were no less than any of us.

I quickly came to realize that God was using me because there were those who could not relate to these men on the level that I could. I had never been homeless, however, my voids and having been repeatedly rejected by others was very similar to elements of their stories. I could relate to their hopelessness alone; thinking that things may never change.

Helping others by validating them is something I have found to be personally rewarding. Sometimes I would see hope in the eyes of these men. Laughing with them as we talked was in its own way a measure of healing. The most surprising thing in working with these men was their interest in the word of God. They made poor choices along the way as we all have. They were regretful. They were lonely, and they wanted their families restored at all cost.

I was able to relate to these men based on the stories they shared of their own family dynamics. These men were some of the most appreciative men I had ever met. Some of them gave new meaning to being respectful. I have learned to be heard is vital to a person's self-worth. I can only imagine if I were ever heard along my life's journey, it would have gained me a measure of self-worth. I would have been better equipped for a society that seems to define you by your shortcomings and deficits.

I was desperate for my mom to have her family in her life the way it was supposed to be. She must have wanted this as well. She never spoke much about it. Her silence didn't protect me emotionally. It caused me to form my own opinion based on my circumstances, and the treatment of others. I was forced to accept that no one cared about my welfare.

My mom deserved a better life than she was granted. She would become invisible in all ways impossible. I used to wonder if my mom's bad health was the result of having one kid after another. My memory although blurry is of my mom bringing my youngest brother home after nearly dying giving birth, due to complications. My parents (these two words would never be in my vocabulary) divorced around this time. I was 7.

Right around this time three men knocked on my door inviting me and my sisters to go to church with them. Strange as this sounds, my mom would ask me and my sisters if we wanted to go, and I clearly remember saying yes. She permitted us to attend. Although, I get chills as I write this part of my story in how I would be introduced to God, I see clearly how God orchestrated those steps of long ago. Allowing three men to take your kids to Church would never happen in today's Society. I would have never allowed this to happen, regardless if it were deemed "safe". This would be the only church I attended throughout my childhood.

Looking back to my humble beginnings, I still have a hard time following God in it all. Being forced to live the way my family had to live, and having God in our lives from the start such as mine seems to be odd or does it. The world chooses those who have something to give; something to gain from others; and their desire is to be with those who can open doors for them. They choose families who are prominent, or those whom they can easily relate to. The list goes on and on.

God from the beginning of time chose those whom the world rejects. He chose the lowly to be his disciples who would be part of the great commission. He sees all that the world sees, and he sees everything else. But he chooses differently than how the world chooses. Makes a lot more sense seeing it from an adults' perspective. I spent my life trying to escape what society would otherwise ignore. My problem was that I looked for those things that society deemed important; polar opposite to what God sees as important. Seeing those who had a high self-esteem based on how they operated in life caused me to what to emulate them for the obvious.

Self-esteem was frowned on when I was a child. It had a different definition years ago. It was associated with pride. Being prideful was definitely frowned upon. I have watched over the years as schools have gone to the extreme to ensure that all kids have "high self-esteem." In some ways this seems to have crippled our young people, or at best made them self-indulgent. Both ends of the spectrum can hurt. For these kids, everything seems to be about them. Therefore, they have no space within themselves to think of others.

As I grew in my relationship with the Lord, his word came to provide me with the correct definition of self-esteem. It is thinking of others as more important than ourselves. Romans 12:3 ESV warns, "Do not think of yourself more highly than you ought, but rather think of yourself with sober judgment, in accordance with the measure of faith God has given you." Our worth and self-esteem is attained by having a right relationship with God. We can know we are valuable because of the unmeasurable high price God paid for us through the blood of his Son Jesus Christ. This should humble true believers.

I recall those who said countless times to me, not to worry, everything will be ok, or promised that things would get better for me. This played out for me as only pretend, providing me with a "temporary" feel-good. A tease that seemed to be part of my DNA. However, God's peace that surpasses all understanding is not pretend, and is not a temporary feel-good or a tease. It's what he gives to his true born-again believers and it is as real as Jesus Christ is, regardless of their circumstances.

I used to think that time will eventually erase all the bad memories of growing up in poverty. Will I ever be able to wrap my head around what life was like for me so long ago. To have been given a measure of understanding of what my mom went through from her own perspective would have helped me. Having more insight into her life would have helped me with the unanswered questions that still haunt me today. How did she keep her secrets locked up inside her all her life?

If she could have sat me down and told me the real dangers of my neighborhood, I am quite sure I would have understood to a degree. Hearing and seeing things that were very foreign to me in my neighborhood, that piqued my curiosity just kept me in the dark. It has taken years for me to understand all that transpired in my growing up years. Did my low self-esteem that kept me so shy and afraid of those around me protect me from engaging in things that I would have lived to regret. My desperation to fit in and my low self-esteem that didn't allow me to join in seems to be a contradiction in terms. Was I inadvertently sabotaging myself without realizing it?

Did my mom inadvertently cause my confusion in her attempts to protect me from the unknowns, those many dangers that were circulating in my neighborhood. I was absolutely a victim in the makings. Not having the God given tools cripples you from seeing both the good and the bad. The fact that my mom in her ongoing bad health had the strength and the fortitude to protect me in her own way says much to me now. The word that comes to mind is true grit, my mom had true grit until her health declined to the degree that she just existed.

I wonder how many times she wanted to give up. I wonder if she ever wished her children weren't born. I wonder if my mom wanted to die at times when she was so sick. She slept so much of the time as her health declined. I wondered if she would ever wake up at times. I would watch her sleep with all the noise from kids running and screaming, and nothing seemed to stir her.

I would climb into bed with her at times and rub her feet. I felt unsafe when she slept so much. My imagination would take me places that scared me even more. If someone came in and took me away, she would never know. How could she protect me then? Given what I lived so close to and the fact that it never touched me physically is a miracle that only God is capable of performing.

Although my mom intervened when I would get too close to the neighbors, she permitted me to help a neighbor out who moved in next door with three little boys. I would play with them at times. Their mom appreciated my help. She loved how I interacted with them. She would leave them locked in their bedrooms by themselves when she went out. I worried about them. They would bang on the window to get my attention. She would always come home, and love all over them. They appeared to be secure.

When I look back, I longed for that same love that this mom gave to her children. Was I so emotionally detached, that my focus was more on the love she gave her three boys, then the potential harm they were in, being locked into a bedroom? Feeling invisible, alone and rejected over time must damage the very core of a person.

Although my mom's insight was incredible as I look back, I didn't make it easy for her. I took it very personally that she kept such a close eye on me when I was outside just jumping rope with the kids on my sidewalk. I felt like a criminal having no idea what I had done wrong. My mom sheltering me to the degree that she did would just fuel my ongoing fears. She wasn't as strict when I was entertaining the neighbors three little boys.

Much of what my mom did to protect me was evident after I grew up. I would figure out much on my own, from reading between the lines. With maturity, I could see her protection from an adult's perspective. However, being left to figure it out on my own wasn't easy. The missing link in all of this is was communication, and intentional love from her that I desperately needed.

My mom could have spared me so much heartache and pain if she told me once in a great while that she loved me. If she would have shared one concern that she had with me, this would have instilled in me a sense of belonging. That would have equated to love for me. If she hugged me once, it would have screamed that she loved me.

When she told me that she was proud of me after I became a mom, I knew she meant it. It was well received, but I didn't require it, as I did when I was that little invisible and lost girl. Rehearsing those words now as an adult helps when I think of her. I can imagine if she would have brought me into her world one time when I was so young, I would have had the permission to tell her how scared I was. I can imagine if I told her how scared I was, she would have potentially hugged me. This would have translated love to me, giving me the confidence that she would protect me. Some of those fears would not have had the hold on me as they did.

Being desperate for love and attention could have gone terribly wrong when I see clearly what was in my view, and where that could have led me long ago when I was an innocent child. Something caused my spirit to convict me to be on my guard around certain individuals, or perhaps it was common sense which is sound judgment in practical matters. Either way I know without a shadow of a doubt that God intervened in my life too many times to count when I was growing up.

CHAPTER 11

HOPELESSNESS

Luke 1:37

Some who have never felt a sense of hopelessness in their lives have no idea the impact it can have on you. As I reminiscence of days long gone, I recall a neighborhood boy who would stop and talk to me when he was out walking. He went to the middle school that I attended. I came to hear that he didn't attend our high school. He told me that he didn't like it, so he quit. I told him to go back and try again. He would go back.

Things were much different back then; families as a whole didn't always know each other personally. This young man actually lived in the area to which the police were called frequently, so I knew that he had it rough. He was quiet and kind and didn't see education as a necessary tool for his future. Back then schools didn't have the programs that could help those who needed assistance with their academics. I wish that I would have had the confidence to help him. My academics came so much easier to me. He apparently had a learning disability. If I had the needed tools back then as I do now, I could have helped him on some level. I never shared the gospel of Jesus Christ with him. Was it because he couldn't comprehend, or was it out of fear? A missed opportunity no matter how you look at it. Did his hopelessness ever change for the better as it did for me?

He eventually quit school and that would be the last time I ever saw him. I felt sorry for him. He seemed so lost. I wonder if this young man was disregarded in his home as he was at school. No one seemed to care about him. Reminds me of the little preschool boy that I tutored that summer. He screamed rejected and alone. Did that little boy grow up to live a life equal to that young man who quit high school before really giving it a try.

Years later I would be watching a documentary about Romania's orphanages. Seeing the overcrowded conditions captivated me. The documentarians apparently were filming the little children when they caught a little boy in a high chair hitting another little boy in the high chair next to him. The little boy cried and cried. What the filmmakers discovered after a time of no one coming to the little boy's rescue is that he stopped crying. When he was hit later, he didn't cry. This went on for some time, absolutely heart-wrenching. I was astonished that those who were filming this documentary did nothing to console this little boy and others like him.

The documentary brought something to my mind. Although there is no real comparison to be made here, I would be reminded in my young life that all I wanted and needed was approval and acceptance. Always dreaming that others would stop rejecting me based on my circumstances. That someone would rescue me and just give me a chance. This desire would absolutely consume me.

I put a great deal of energy into desiring, hoping, and praying that the rejection from others would cease. Finding no cessation to any of the negative things in my life, I began to give up. I see now that I didn't just give up, as my hope diminished over time; I became invisible. When others hurt me because they simply could, I never discussed it or addressed it for most of my life. Unbeknownst to me, I just stuffed it.

I never told my mom all those scary things that happened to me. I never shared with her my own personal fears of the unknown, and the real fears that I faced. I wonder if the reason I didn't tell her is the same reason why that precious little boy stopped crying because he had been forced to come to the realization subconsciously that his crying didn't matter. No one seemed to be listening. He was a toddler; he didn't understand. He couldn't talk, however something told him that his pain was not going to stop, so why cry. How profoundly sad.

Although I am fully aware how blessed this nation is compared to the rest of the world, I give myself permission to call my life what it was, and to validate my feelings based on my own life's circumstances for once in my life. It is vital to my healing as I would learn so many years later. Stuffing it is just another form of crippling that can prevent necessary healing. It is also vital to recognize and come to terms with what happened to me along my life's journey. The alternative is to stay in denial and sweep the hurts under a rug minimizing all that occurred.

To speak of the negative things that happened to me is much healthier than to never to speak of it as I did throughout my life. Watching the wounds that never heal fester and bleed until I am forced to call it what it is. Carrying wounds into every relationship is a constant reminder that you are less than everyone else. This mindset can prevent a person from becoming all that God has called him or her to be.

Others who would speak for me, refer to me, or condemn me for finally recognizing my hurts, my voids, and my disappointments that crippled me were the very ones whom I allowed to have such a hold on me that kept me in the same place emotionally, psychologically, and mentally. This ongoing behavior would bring suicide to my mind. God is the only one who has the power to create life, and the only one who has the right to take it. Therefore, suicide is never an option. The point here is the pain that one human-being can bestow upon another human-being can be devastating.

I kept my life experiences a secret to protect myself emotionally. To finally speak of it and be condemned was just about the last straw for me. My God said no when I personally thought death was the only answer. My God said no to me living a life being constantly controlled by others. My God said no to me being defined by others, as a result of how I was forced to live as a child that left me a shell of a person.

Unfortunately, the deep wounds and deficits would come into play when you least expect it. When you exit your childhood thinking that was then, and this is now, only to be quickly reminded that those unfilled voids left in your childhood prevents you from successfully moving forward to the next chapter of your life. It secures your failures. Lacking the basics tools to enter adulthood is one thing, embarking on a marriage a week after turning 18 is quite another.

Hiding issues that were never addressed only worked for a time. Sweeping them under a rug was simply a Band-Aid, a temporary fix. Some good times were thrown into the mix, but these would prove to be yet another temporary fix. Years and years would go by with both good times, and bad times. Problems never fixed and the stresses of life would bring the past to life.

Discontentment and unhappiness as a result of bad behavior would begin to surface on a larger scale. The past hurts never got resolved so that healing could take place. Not a bit of self-esteem to defend. Fear setting in that could potentially prevent my children's needs from being met took immediate precedence. I couldn't imagine them having to repeat my childhood. It wasn't up for debate. Trying to play both parents only worked in a superficial way. Children need a strong hand to guide them, and unconditional love poured upon them. They need approval and a listening ear.

Children need support, not just when they are little, cute, and adorable, but also when they are big, not so cute, and obnoxious! Children need a Godly man as a father, not just to provide for them, but also to pour into them the truth of Gods' word. Simply living under the same roof became the norm. Silence equated to deafness. God would prove to me along the way that material things are never a substitute for emotional needs. I say this based on my experience as a child growing up in poverty; and I was poor in every sense of the word.

CHAPTER 12

HEALING WOULD BEGIN

Revelation 21:4

How is it possible for a person who comes into the world to grow up so devoid of all the necessary vital tools that should otherwise sustain, find herself one day actually making it, weathered and torn without a doubt, but still making it, and in some ways smelling like a rose, not the most fragrant rose, and not a high-end rose, but a rose nonetheless? How do you make something out of nothing?

To be born with mental handicaps is one thing. To be born with all the abilities that are needed for your own personal growth at every stage of life, but not have them ever come to fruition will never make sense to me. The many unfortunate circumstances I found myself in from being ill-equipped in vital stages of life ended up crippling me. This seems absolutely senseless.

To ignore the voids in children and sit idly by doing nothing is heartless. To do nothing leaves an innocent child falling behind in every area of development that will adversely affect the child for life. Even those who seemingly do find paths that lead them onto a better road are still left with wounds that never seem to totally heal, with a flood of memories that are absolutely heart breaking.

How does one survive emotionally, psychologically, or mentally with a background such as mine? I am fully aware that there are those who have had it worse than I have. This fact doesn't negate a lifetime of voids so deep that are never addressed. You find yourself playing catch-up the rest of your life.

I personally could not have made it without God. There were times when I question whether or not I actually have made it. I say this because of the memories of long ago that can set you back when you let your guard down. The constant memories and the real fear that I would have to go back and live there one day can paralyze on a different level.

Those who held me down, who gave me morsels of hope, but just enough to keep me from truly being victorious in my life kept me stuck. I began to fear later in life that my children would have to taste similar experiences to mine. There were times when it seemed to be more than I could bear.

I wonder what could have change my destiny here on earth? Being born into another family? Being adopted? If my mom had married someone who belonged to God Almighty? Someone noticing my family's living conditions and having a heart to help? If my mom had a family that was supportive and loving?

God didn't cause the circumstances that created the voids within me that not only crippled me, but could have and should have killed me. God is in control of all things. He could have delivered me from it all. He performs miracles every day. His word says that he loves the entire world. Surely the entire world includes me. My own world never seemed to include me. My world said to me loud and clear by way of their actions, and deeds, that I was far from being equal to them. I wasn't even in the same ballpark with them socially, intellectually, financially or even spiritually. No one in my own world ever truly loved me, unless I had something to give them, or do for them.

I learned that my Lord and Savior loves me unconditionally. He has my name written in the Lamb's book of life. No one can take me out of my Father's hand. My Savior is preparing a place for me in heaven where I will reign with him for all eternity. This I know with certainty. I don't have to work for it, earn it, or buy it. Salvation is a free gift to all who heed Gods' call on their life.

God's truth is that I needed a Savior. And Jesus Christ, the one true God of the Universe died for me and arose the third day. Now this is love. God did it all for me, and now he works mightily in me. He gets all credit, glory, praise and adoration for who he is in my life. All I had to do was accept his free gift of salvation, no strings attached, no teasing, no working, no begging, and no sorrow. "No strings attached was icing on the cake for me."

I now see that God knew precisely what I would go through, and although he didn't choose the countless hurts I would endure, he allowed them because he knew that he would ultimately use my heartaches in life to grow me closer to him.

He knew what I could handle, and he knew exactly what I couldn't handle. He has proven to me over and over that I can do all things through Christ who strengthens me. I may appear to be a slow learner, but I am exactly where my God wants me. I will be victorious because the Holy Spirit is working in me to make me what God has called me to be.

Society screams loud and clear, it's who you know, and who knows you that matters in this world. I spent my life longing to be that person. To have known someone who could give a helping hand, or be known by someone who could have opened a door that I had no hope in opening for myself was a wish that never came true for me. I had to grow up Spiritually to see that I did in fact know of someone, and I am personally known by him, Jesus Christ God Almighty! John 10:14 "ESV" I am the good shepherd, and I know my own, and my own know me.

My problem was that I put my hope in mankind. I tried to pay my way with my actions, and deeds, looking to belong, to fit in, to be liked, and to be noticed. I wanted an ounce of attention. I had my fair share of being constantly ostracized and rejected. Fighting my own battles, or attempting too was a dead end again and again. With no one to help me, I eventually shut down. I found myself crippled, helpless, and hopeless. I became a shell of a person. I somehow came to the conclusion that I had to do things on my own since those in my own world were silent.

I depended on mankind instead of leaving it all in God's hands. I allowed my thoughts to captivate me and my circumstances to define me, all because of the constant lack of hope I had in every area of my life.

I pray that God will take "From poverty to riches in Christ Jesus" and deposit it in the hands of someone who can relate to my life up to now. The bible says that God holds us accountable for what we do know; he doesn't hold us accountable for what we do not know. He knew that I was a victim in this fallen world. He knew that my flesh could not endure all that was bestowed upon me. He knew that I needed him in every facet of my life, even when I wasn't aware of my need. He also knew that I was innocent and equally ignorant to what was before and around me. Yes, he allowed me to endure all that I did so that I could give him all credit, glory, and praise for choosing me as his own.

God uses all things in our lives, the good, the bad and the ugly to show us who he is in us for his greater purpose in our lives, which is to conform us to his Son.

God's promise never to leave us or forsake us is written in his blood which he shed on the cross of Calvary. His DEATH, BURIAL and RESURRECTION is all the hope we will ever need when he calls us to repentance, acknowledging that he is LORD of all lords and KING of all kings over our lives.

If I were given the opportunity to choose my path in life as a child, I absolutely would not have chosen what I have lived through. If I had known what my life would look like as a child prior to me experiencing it, my flesh would have chosen death. If God would have shown me the life I would live as a child knowing that I belonged to him; I pray that I would have willingly obeyed, trusting him with all of me. Now that I am far away from the life I lived as a child, I realize that God will always be in control.

I see those without Christ being crippled and voided to the degree that I was, even though their worlds were polar opposite to mine. Their voids in their lives that resulted in them being crippled is profoundly different. Their money, fame, families, friends, freedom, self-esteem, power, higher education, electronics and bells and whistles of every kind is a smoke screen to the one thing they need most, a relationship with Jesus Christ. And one day, every knee shall bow to him and every tongue will confess that Jesus Christ is LORD.

To be totally clueless as a result of the countless voids in you, that leads to being crippled is horrible. To be spiritually clueless, having no idea how crippled you really are is much worse. It will be forever separated from God, in hell for all eternity. Which option would one choose when it's presented this way?

What God has done for me in tangible ways just adds to my testimony. He has permitted me to live in safe places ever since I entered adulthood. He has given me opportunities such as higher education, learning about the world in which I live in, things that I didn't know were possible for me. Those things I had no chance of gaining on my own.

College wasn't an option for me when I graduated high school. Attending college in my early forties to become an R.N. was very rewarding to me. My passion was for the elderly for obvious reasons. Older people are in many ways forgotten, and many are abused because they have no voice to defend themselves as they age. We have the tendency to forget the legacies that the older generations have played in paving the way for the next generation. Although I can't relate to those who had extended families, I have watched many who can relate.

I'm sure not having an extended family when I was young didn't help the life I had to live. I used to dream of having grandparents. Perhaps God wants me to remember where I came from so that I will not take for granted where I am now.

I want my life to be a testimony of how God works in the lives of his true born-again believers no matter what challenges they are up against. I equally want my life to be a testimony to those who see clearly Gods' hand of protection over his true believers.

What a testimony for those who are desperately in need of seeing that only God can fill the voids in our lives. The all too familiar fleeting pleasures the world offers will always leave them discontent. This doesn't allow them to experience the peace and lasting joy that our souls crave. The truth is the world can't give what God can only give.

The most important and most vital life-and-death lesson that took nearly a lifetime to learn, is just how much my Lord and Savior Jesus Christ loves me. Jesus paid a debt he could never owe, and every single person that God created owes a debt they will never be able to pay. Romans 5:8 NIV "But God demonstrates his own love for us in this: while we were still sinners, Christ died for us." I didn't have to gain approval first. I didn't have to work to achieve. He loved me first.

If I would have had ears to hear from the start, I can imagine that I would have dealt with my life circumstances differently. I still would have cried a river of tears at times. I still would have been hungry at times. I still would have been scared at times, and even scared to death at times. I still would have cried out to God the same way. I still would have been unfairly dealt with at times. I still would have been treated unkindly at times. I still would have been frightened by bullies, although I would have realized that they were just bullies with no power, which would have definitely softened the blow.

I still would have failed as often. I still would have worried myself sick about my mom. I still would have felt the sting of others ostracizing me. I still would have had to deal with those who teased me relentlessly. I still would have been forced to deal with all the injustices without a voice to fight back. I still would have been rejected. I still would have been marginalized by the world.

The difference would have been that I would have personally known God's peace that surpasses all understanding, and I mean all of it! I would have personally known God's unspeakable joy. I can see the benefit of that now. I would have depended on God for my mere existence, instead of depending on my own efforts, which I realized I didn't even possess. I would have grown in my walk with the Lord, instead of wanting to evaporate from this earth as a result of others and myself failing me.

I depended on people against all hope, and I depended on myself against all hope. People will fail us even with good intentions. God never fails us. He will not push to get himself a place in our hearts. He patiently waits until we invite him in. We must get out of the way, and allow the Holy Spirit to guide and direct us. God will always be with us and whatever we are asked to do, for whatever trial we may face, we have the assurance that we are never alone. And one day as we are faithfully going along according to Gods' Sovereign Will, we will begin to see just how much God is growing us in his word.

When this happens, our prayer life becomes more meaningful, and we find ourselves gaining an insatiable appetite for God's word. Our walk with him continues to grow, and in time we find ourselves desiring to be in constant fellowship with him. The only reason we would ever want to look back to the difficult times is to be reminded of all that he has done in our lives that has brought us to where we are now.

I have come to the realization that I would rather depend on God for my every need than to have a million dollars in my bank account on which I am forced to depend on. I have tasted and seen that the Lord is good, and I have tasted and felt his hand of protection over me unequivocally.

Luke 18:17 "NIV" says, Truly I tell you, anyone who will not receive the kingdom of God like a little child, will never enter it. This verse was taught to me by my teachers of long ago.

I gladly accept that God made the message of Salvation so simple that even a child can comprehend it. Children are teachable and humble. We don't need to be Theologians to comprehend everything about Salvation. After all, God is the one opening our Spiritual eyes to see his truth. He chose us before the foundation of the world. In addition to God making the Salvation message simple for those who have ears to hear, he equally made it so complex that no atheist has ever been able to solve the puzzle unequivocally.

God who spoke the world into existence makes him the author and owner of everything that exists. Our God-given free Will allows us the freedom to accept or reject this truth. Rejecting it doesn't make it any less true, any more than believing it makes it false.

The Bible is clear with countless verses that make the point that the truth of the word of God is not up for intellectual debate. The truth of God's word is for those who believe and see their need for a Savior; believing that Jesus Christ is the only true and living God of the universe, and recognizing his sacrifice on the cross for all mankind. We may either accept Christ or reject him.

Faith is a free gift from God himself. We don't have to comprehend everything about God, as we can't. To say otherwise is to make him smaller than he is. No words in any language will ever be able to truly express or define his majesty. This simply says it all.

When we attempt to figure out God on our own, by means of human intellect, human reasoning, or human technology, we fail simply because that is not the way God intended it to be. When we believe by the faith God gives us and begin to live by the faith God gives us, he begins to reveal himself to those who are truly his.

This truth is evident in my life, when I step back and look at what God has done, and is doing in my life. In spite of me, in spite of bad choices I made, and despite that I did things on my own; my God has been faithful and forgiving. I have found myself sobbing my eyes out which has quickly brought back memories of me sobbing my eyes out as a child, only to discover that the two examples of sobbing have nothing to do with each other.

I have a testimony to share with those who can relate to me, based on their own life experiences and unfortunate circumstances that left them with their own personal heartache, and disappointments that seemed to last a lifetime.

Depending on a world in which I lived out my life trying to understand and fit in kept me in a fog. With the ongoing consequences of working independently against all hope never allowed things to get better. Any "successes" would prove to be fleeting at best, again and again.

I used to think, where did I go wrong? What was missing that I needed the approval, acceptance and love of those who crossed my path. At what point did I think more of the opinion of those in my own little world than I did of Gods' opinion of me? I was in church where I heard clearly and repeatedly that God loved me unconditionally.

What was the missing link that led me to choose the world over God, even after having his truth inside me.? Was my knowledge of God merely head knowledge? Could it be the fact that there was no difference between my peers at church, and my classmates at school? The kids at church and camp excluded me, ignored me, and never gravitated to me, equal to the experiences I had with my classmates in public school.

My lack of things screamed loud and clear that I was odd. My social economic situation was the reason I couldn't have material things. Superficial as they are, I felt cheated and alone. No one could have convinced me otherwise. It caused me much heartache and pain when I compared myself to those who were from families with financial gain.

It wasn't only about me coveting what they had. Much of my heartache was how society held my deficits against me, and it materialized in how I was treated, ignored and disrespected. This is still so vivid in my memory. It takes me back with clarity to where I had to live so long ago. Not a good feeling.

How much of what my peers did to me was done simply out of ignorance, no fault of their own. Is it fair of me to judge them based on their behavior? Were they as innocent as I was? Were their parents to blame? Is society to blame?

2nd Peter 1:5-7 NIV says "For this very reason, make every effort to add to your faith goodness, and to goodness knowledge, and to knowledge self-control, and to self-control perseverance, and to perseverance Godliness, and to Godliness mutual affection, and to mutual affection, love.

Got it! Now what do I do with this knowledge that is supposed to be for my good. How was I to make sense of it all when the kids at church were no different than the kids in my neighborhood or at my public school. The kids in my church read these same verses! We were all taught to obey God in all things. We were taught that God loves us the same. We were taught to help others. We were taught to pray for each other. We were taught to forgive. We were taught to be kind. I remind myself that we are all fallen people in a fallen world, and that our flesh chooses not to obey God's commandments at times, and indeed fights them daily, if not hourly. I get this.

Where was that one person in my life, that one kid who looked past my dirty appearance and my socio-economic situation. That one person who not only didn't care about my humble beginnings, but was willing to give me a chance. I would have understood if my peers had given me a chance, and decided they didn't like my personality, or my behavior. I have come to think as hurtful, and painful as that would have been, at least I would have known the reason. The facts have always screamed loud and clear their reasons for rejecting and ostracizing me. As I look back, I am confident that it had nothing to do with my personality or my behavior.

Hearing repeatedly how lucky I was to live in the United States, and that there were others who had it so much worse, not only in Third World Countries, but in my own back yard, didn't help eradicate my pain, or change my destiny.

Learning the difference of belonging to a society in this life, and belonging to God where I would spend eternity after this life ends, reminds me what is important. The two worlds would be polar opposite to each other. As a child I didn't have a clue. What a Revelation it would be for me nearly a lifetime later.

What came first. My unrealistic desire to be like everyone else based on what I was forced to see day in and day out, or the lack of the crucial tools that is required to move forward in life that I wasn't granted. It doesn't matter at this point. I am still breathing and God is the reason. That's a testimony.

CHAPTER 13

GRATITUDE

1 Thessalonians 5:18

When I take a moment and step out of the world that I lived in as a child, and take a look from the outside looking in, I am quickly reminded of what my Sunday school teachers did for me. I would be invited to a girls' bible study once a week after school. My bible teacher was different than many of the teachers at school. She didn't favor any of us over the other. She didn't judge me because I couldn't relate to others who had their needs met. She didn't single anyone out who had more to offer. She never left me out. She treated us all equally. She would make us feel special by allowing us to have a soda while we were listening to her teach us the bible. This may have been the tip of the iceberg of being introduced to what fairness looked and felt like. This experience unfortunately would turn out to be bittersweet for me as the result of not personally experiencing it much of the time.

My teacher would ask questions in relation to her lesson. One day she asked if any of us knew Jesus as our Savior. After a time went by and no one answered, she turned to me in front of the other girls and ask if I had accepted Jesus in my heart. My shyness never allowed me to answer any of her questions about our lesson. I was even more unprepared to answer that question. Being the only Caucasian girl at the bible study made me even more shy. I just looked down, and my teacher said with such kindness in her voice, that she knew that I was saved. I was now embarrassed. I sure didn't feel "saved".

One day she took us out to a restaurant to have lunch. For some reason I couldn't join the others in ordering a complete meal with a drink and dessert. I would have a sandwich and water, no dessert. I remember being annoyed and confused as to why I didn't order what I really wanted to eat. Outings to restaurants were not the norm for me. Believe me when I say that I desired French fries, a soda, and dessert so much so that my tongue was hanging out; just to make my point here.

I would feel my insides welling up with more annoyance when some of the girls wasted their food. Whereas, I ate every crumb of my sandwich. I felt my mom sitting on my shoulder and watching me. If I had taken advantage of my teacher, that would not have sat well with her. I can promise you one thing, I wanted more!

Years later I would reconnect with this teacher. We began to reminisce of long ago. We talked about the bible study she taught in my neighborhood. She said although I was so shy, she knew that there was something special about me. I regret not asking her to elaborate. I was still the same shy person to some degree. We were having lunch and the story of the restaurant came up. We began reminiscing of that experience. She wondered why I didn't order what I wanted. Eventually I would tell her that perhaps it was because my mom had so little, and no one took her out to eat. My teacher was sad that my circumstances never changed when I was growing up. She was thankful to the Lord that he delivered me from the life I lived as a child. She knew first hand how I lived. She visited our apartment countless times.

Her words would come to my mind years later as I was writing down my thoughts. Reliving those words spoken to me with such tenderness has touched me dearly. Things were much different back then than they are today. Most people didn't get involved in each other's lives on a personal level. I shared with her that I found it hard to enjoy things that wasn't afforded to my mom. In addition, I didn't want to take advantage of her. I don't remember my mom ever telling me not to take advantage of anyone. I was either born that way, or my low self-esteem played out in a way that prevented me from feeling worthy of gaining things from others. I was equally afraid that I might do something wrong, and embarrass my mom.

One of the family's at my church owned a bible book store. They would pick me up from my apartment, and gave me little jobs to do at the store. This book store was on a level all on its own. It was packed from ceiling to floor with countless books, bibles, and bible material. They had shelves filled to the brim with little novelties, all relating to the bible. I haven't experienced anything like it to this day. They gave all the children in our church bibles, and put our name on them. They allowed us to pick a novelty from the basket on our birthday. Something so small that seemed so big at the time.

I wish that I had the tools to convey to my Sunday school teachers my gratitude for what they did for me from time to time. I was super shy as I reminisce of long ago. I was equally easily embarrassed. Having no self-esteem and no confidence doesn't seem to give you permission to speak freely. You just stay invisible. Their rewards are in Heaven for their consistent obedience in pouring the truth of Gods' word into so many children.

They never knew the real me. I never allowed anyone to get too close. I had nothing to give, so I just stayed inside myself. I never realized to not speak of one's past would result in stuffing all the hurts, and disappointments that described my life as a child growing up in a government housing development. I equally never realized gaining the courage to speak up in written form as I have done would begin such a healing process. Having zero self-esteem doesn't set you up for success on any level as I lived out. Unfortunately, not having even a measure of self-esteem doesn't protect you from those who size you up for their own motives. Some unfortunately will use your insecurities against you for their own personal gain. This can materialize in vile ways.

Living in a fallen world with people who are just looking for an easy target to misuse and emotionally abuse creates in you a victim that you didn't sign up for. But it wasn't until years later that I came to learn what being a victim really meant. I never connected the word *victim* to myself until recently. The concept arose while I was writing my story. The facts always screamed loud to me that I was as much a victim, as I had been born into poverty. I just didn't attach myself to that word until the facts wouldn't allow me to be in denial anymore.

Chronological age comes into play whether one is emotionally ready or not. Being encouraged to grow spiritually as you grow chronologically is normal. As you grow chronologically, but aren't given the time to grow emotionally, you play catch-up. Staying behind emotionally while growing chronologically is obviously backwards. This isn't normal. This can hurt you on the same magnitude as living in constant fear. Both prevents you from learning and growing to your fullest potential. Growing up immature can cause you to make decisions that you wouldn't otherwise make.

I may have been emotionally young for my age, but God in his grace protected me when I grew up from believing things said in churches that weren't scriptural. If it doesn't line up with scripture, it should be thrown out, regardless if it makes you feel good, tickles your ears, or gives you a sense of security. Although God permitted me to be behind emotionally, he protected me where it matters most.

Only the truth of God's word will grow a person spiritually. If there is a small crack in your heart causing you to hear anything that is contrary to the word of God, this gives the enemy a landing spot. He will come into your head and slowly and gradually distort the truth of God's word. One of the ways a small crack can develop is when a human viewpoint comes into play that is not based on scripture.

As we read in 2nd Timothy 4:3 NIV "For the time will come when people will not put up with sound doctrine. Instead, to suit their desires they will gather around them a great number of teachers to say what there itching ears want to hear".

Jesus walked on the earth preaching his truth to those who had ears to hear his truth. As I continued to understand his word, I could see that he chose ordinary people to spread the truth of God's word. I heard this as a child with no reaction. I read it now for myself and it consoles my soul that I serve a Risen Savior that doesn't judge the outward appearance or the status of a person.

Once again, I would see the difference of how God operates and how society operates. Both ends of the spectrum if you will. I spent my life chasing what society deemed important. I wanted God and I wanted to fit in society simultaneously. I wanted to emulate others; it seemed to work for them, why not me? I wanted Gods' truth. I wanted to learn about him. I wanted to obey him, even when I questioned him at times. I didn't have the ability to make sense of the confusion, the heartaches, and the ongoing never-ending circumstances that plagued me. Years later, I would come to the realization just how blessed I was to be taught Gods' truth by true believers so long ago.

CHAPTER 14

WORSHIP IN SONGS

Colossians 3:16

My "church" was plain and simple. It did have a piano; and those who could sing. I represented the young people who would sing their lungs out no matter the pitch. Equally as memorable is that many songs we sang were hymns written from scripture. Unfortunately, I didn't appreciate this to the appreciable degree until I grew up and visited other churches who couldn't hold a candle to what I experienced as a child. In many churches today if a church service doesn't have all the bells and whistles, it is deemed as boring, unloving, and on some levels legalistic. If the music is not on par with that which the world offers, it is deemed as not true worshipping of God to its fullest. The songs we would sing praised and glorified God. Many songs we sang were word for word from the bible.

The definition of *worship* from scripture entails growth in God, revering who he is, honoring him, and bringing glory to his name in all our actions, words and deeds 24/7.

It's simply "singing" if the effort is based entirely on emotions. Emotions are a part of who we are in Christ Jesus, and music can and does create an atmosphere that honors God. The lyrics alone can bring glory and praise to his name. Many churches today see the music as everything, and it supersedes the word of God.

The word of God in its entirety brings the glory due to God Almighty. The truth of God's word convicts, humbles, forgives, grows us spiritually, and equips us to be the light and witness of the truth of God's word to a spiritually blind and spiritually dying world.

Gods' word causes us to become mature in Christ Jesus. "Yet a time is coming and has now come when the true worshippers will worship the Father in spirit and in truth, for they are the kind of worshipers the Father seeks". John 4:23 NIV True worship must be in "spirit" that is engaging the whole heart. Having a passion and knowledge of the God we worship in spirit and in truth is evident of who we are in Christ Jesus.

Worship must be vital and real in the heart to materialize in our actions, words, and our deeds. Emotions without all of God's truth produces a life void of his truth. The essence of true worship is not only external but also internal. It materializes in our lives as our obedience is aligned to the entire word of God. Finding ourselves not desiring all of Gods' truth will cause us to not see him clearly. If we don't realize it sooner than later, we will find ourselves not under the umbrella of God.

Our flesh begins to take over, resulting in our emotions controlling us. We begin in inchworm process to accept things that we would not have accepted when we were under the umbrella of God. We all can justify our behavior at any given moment. If what we do is contrary to the word of God, we are guilty of disobeying him. Allowing my emotions to control me manifested itself differently causing me to depend on mankind, that unfortunately would derail me at times. This cost me sweet fellowship with God. In his grace, he protected me from falling headlong.

This mindset made such an impact on me, that I am still recovering today, trying to wrap my head around my decision to give up, as opposed to taking advantage of my Lord and Savior who lived inside my heart to fight all my battles. Every aspect of where I am now is polar opposite to where I was as a child, and it shakes my entire being when I think that the only tool that I ever needed was Jesus, and he was in arm's length of me, and I didn't utilize him one single bit.

Well may I say that I am making up for lost time. I allowed Satan the father of lies, the accuser, the slanderer, the evil one, to use my circumstances against me when I was growing up. However, God's hand of protection was all over me as evidence that Satan didn't win. Indeed, he will never win against God's true believers.

Although I had it down pat who I had been made to be by society's standards, I wasn't that person. I am not that person now. I am equally confident of who I am now, a child of the KING of all kings, LORD of all lords; a princess no less, chosen by the only true and living God of the universe.

I am encouraged because the power of God's promises and his faithfulness to keep those promises are written in stone. Psalm 32:8 NIV says " I will instruct you and teach you in the way you should go; I will counsel you with my loving eye on you" This verse speaks to me even more as I study his word. I can believe that the power of Gods promises is true; and I can trust him to keep his promises to me on a personal level.

Why didn't I allow this verse to be planted in my heart so I could have experienced Gods' peace on a regular basis. Equally, how did I allow my deficits to follow me into my adulthood? If I had known that there would be those who would begin where others had stopped, I could have been better prepared, and the false sense of security that I thought I gained would not have set me back emotionally. No amount of pleading, begging, working, or obeying gave me an ounce of hope.

Perhaps I was continually looking for the world's security and not Gods' iron clad guarantee. The world promise's is never a guarantee and will always fail us. What God promises even though we don't yet see is something we can believe and live by. The confidence that it will become a reality because we serve the God of all Creation who said it, and that settles it for me.

I went through life believing a lie that only the elite have gifts with which to serve God. I accepted this lie. Until I grew up and had a desire to work with children, I realized how easy it came to me, and the joy that came from teaching children Gods' word. Parents would share with me that bed time was difficult in their home except for Saturday night when the children realized that they were going to get to see Ms. Sharyn the next day at church. Although this would warm my heart, I never made much out of it. As a matter of fact, this is one of the few times I have mentioned it. My interests in spending time with kids came so natural to me.

Subconsciously I wanted my mom to do things with me that I did for my own children and other kids. I wanted my mom to read to me. I wanted her to do art projects with me. I wanted to converse with my mom. I just wanted to be noticed, to be told verbally that I am loved and that I am special. Perhaps I would not have been so focused on society's opinion of me. This assurance would have made a difference in how I lived out my childhood and young adulthood emotionally. I waited for my mom to tell me that she loved me. Years would come and go. Why didn't I say those words to her first? Was it the same reason that I never ask anyone for help?

I told my kids that I loved them in every way possible. We would even do sign language when we were in places where we couldn't talk. I prepared them for what was in store for them each school year. I physically watched them do their homework when they were in elementary school. I went to every school event. Their teachers knew that I was a phone call away.

I do recall my mom helping me prepare for an history exam that I was struggling with before her health dictated her life in those early years. I knew that my mom was innately smart. She didn't have the home life that would have afforded her the needed encouragement, and opportunities needed to succeed. The many obstacles that plagued her over the course of her adult life stunted her on all levels. I don't blame her and I never did.

What I needed to finally accept was the fact that my mom was never able to be there for me emotionally or physically. Saying it seemed to be a judgment against her. I have never walked in her shoes and therefore I can't begin to judge her. I always knew that she wasn't able to be the mom she wanted to be.

My devotion to her came from gaining the knowledge that painted more of a clear picture of her life so long ago. I began to see the bigger picture when I was becoming healthier emotionally. I never knew how to defend myself or share with my mom my true feelings. Obviously, I didn't have the permission that I needed to see things from my own perspective. The hard-core facts of my experiences were never defined for me personally. I was always in the dark until I grew up figuring it out on my own.

In order to heal you must acknowledge, and to acknowledge, you must choose to forgive, and choosing to forgive, you must recognize the real pain, as too not find yourself reliving the deep-seated hurts that crippled you in all areas of your life. That, which has the potential to take you emotionally right back where you came from. Without God leading and guiding me from my beginning to where I am now, I would cease to exist.

CHAPTER 15

PERSONAL JOURNEY CONTINUES

Deuteronomy 31:6

Separating my relationship with God and my relationship with the world is obvious. Separating my relationship with God and my relationship with other believers has been the hardest mountain to climb for me. And I own it. Jesus is the mediator between God and man, not mankind.

I used to wonder why didn't God fill those crucial voids in my life. Those deep seeded voids that made me play catch-up my entire life. Those voids that kept me stuck and prevented me from going forward in life as others did. Those voids that were defined by others. Those voids that blinded me to my God given talents. Those voids that gave toxic people permission to use me. Those voids that caused me to accept being a doormat. Those voids that caused me to question Gods' love for me. Those voids that killed my self-esteem before I experienced it for myself.

Not self-absorbed "self-esteem" that society has come to embrace. The self-esteem that gives you the drive to be your best where it matters, to do your best when it counts, and to believe that you are worthy on some level. The self-esteem that protects you from being used and abused by those who see you as weak and helpless. The self-esteem that reminds you that the God of the Universe made you in his image, and you too are equally loved and special in his eyes.

God is not responsible or to blame. He entrusts us with parents, giving them the responsibility to raise their children for his glory. Fallen people in a fallen world. Got it! If everyone lived my story, we could all relate and be on the same page. We would all notice each other without glaring. That's a given.

What would it look like for someone who couldn't relate, but noticed the hopelessness in that one person? Instead of turning a blind eye or a deaf ear, they could give a measure of help to that one person, potentially changing the direction of their life. I could imagine that such a life change for that one person would result in changing a life in another person, thus changing the world one person at a time.

I was alone in my own little world helpless with no one to help me, whereas society in large stared right through me, walked right past me, and turned a blind eye and a deaf ear right in front of me.

How in the world did I escape those many dangers? When I think of those dangers that I am personally aware of; I wonder how many more dangers God protected me from that I am not aware of. It absolutely overwhelms me when I try and wrap my mind around it. Over the years I would begin to comprehend the definition of fear, and how that word itself impacted me most of my life. I would learn what a healthy fear looks like or "reverence" in relation to God. The bible says in Proverbs 1:7 (ESV) "The fear of the LORD is the beginning of knowledge."

To reverence God is to respect him, be in awe of him. It's not meant to scare us, as my definition of fear did over my life. Reverence and fear before the one true God of the Universe is not to be taken lightly. Fearing God is having such a reverence for him that it has a great impact on the way we live our lives while on this earth. A life lived in obedience to a Holy God is crucial and should not be taken for granted. For he will judge all mankind when we stand before him and give an account of how we lived our lives for him.

My definition of fear got misplaced as a child. Pain, hurt, and disappointments equated to fear that kept me stuck. People trying to physically hurt me scared me. I was scared because my mom was sick all the time. I was scared that I would anger my mom. I was scared because my mom continued to smoke after she had a lung removed. I was scared for being mad at my mom for sitting on the stoop late at night. I was scared for being mad at my mom because she didn't notice that I needed her. I was scared that she would die when I was so mad at her. I wanted a clean slate in case she died abruptly. My mom didn't hug me as I saw other moms hug their children. I longed for that. I still have a deep longing for my mom to hug me. There are times when I beg God to hug me. There have been times when I pray that I would sense his presence, and his peace seems to flow over me.

I don't hold a grudge against my mom, and I don't hold her accountable because you can only give what you have. I see clearly to blame my mom all those years later would have crippled me in yet another way, and perhaps, the cycle of poverty would not have been broken in my own family. Not that I did anything to "break" the cycle of poverty. I just had so many more opportunities than my mom had. It is only by Gods' grace that I didn't repeat my childhood heartaches. It is only by Gods' mercy that I am not reliving my childhood physically. So, to judge my mom would be a disrespect to my God who has delivered me from a life that could have been worse. A life that for some in my neighborhood never escaped from.

I am still forced to see later in life, just how much a lifestyle of emptiness, voicelessness, helplessness, and hopelessness with no way out will forever be etched in my mind, no matter what has changed over the course of my life up to now. What I have done with it is key. Not me 'per se' but what I have allowed God to do even with my kicking and screaming at times. He has made the difference of me failing, and finding myself slowing becoming a whole person in all areas of my life one small step at a time.

The real hurts and the real pain that comes from being born into poverty can either make us or break us. Without God I would have been a statistic, this I am sure of. With God, not only am I not a statistic, but I am victorious because of who I am in Christ alone. I find myself reacting in shock when I learn that people live this life alone without Christ by their own omission. I am astonished by how many do in fact make it. I see the money, the drugs of choice, and the family support to name a few, that seem to work for such people for a time. I also see the path they are on and the end result will not only be bad, it will be horrendous when they realize the lives that they lived on earth were void of the truth of Jesus Christ. This will result in a total separation from the ONE whom they rejected. There are only two places that will remain in existence once this life on earth is over, Heaven and Hell. We don't have to choose Hell; we just have to reject Heaven by our own free Will.

Perhaps the horrendous life I lived as a child has much to do with my life now as a follower of Jesus Christ. Not to imply that only the "poor" go to heaven. *Poor* used in reference to God has a different meaning. To be poor in spirit is to recognize fully our utter spiritual bankruptcy before God. It is to understand that we have absolutely nothing of worth to offer God. I can surely relate to this on a deep level. We can't do anything to earn, work for, or deserve God's salvation.

I learned later in life as I began with baby steps maturing in my walk with the Lord Jesus that no matter our status in life, we all must recognize our need for Jesus Christ. This idea consoles my soul because when I was a child I had absolutely nothing to give to earn Gods' favor. Coming to Jesus in faith to receive his free gift of salvation without strings attached seemed too good to be true.

Unfortunately, when I was a young adult, my focus was still on mankind. I allowed many people to dictate my worth, and many of these people saw me as worthless. I was so empty that I looked for anyone to help me avoid the pitfalls of life. This only opened doors for the wrong people to find me and use me. I thought if I would have had a friend who protected me, I could have gained the needed tools that would have allowed me to protect myself. God would help me see years later that looking to mankind was not going to give me the hope I needed. I wanted anything by anyone who could have gotten me out of a life that seemed to be printed on my very soul *"This is as good as it gets for me"*.

To hear that it is really a good thing to be "poor in spirit" didn't compute in my mind. I had dreamt my whole life that I wouldn't be poor, would not be without, and would not be so empty. Jesus says, "Blessed are the poor in spirit, for theirs is the kingdom of heaven," meaning that before any of us can enter God's kingdom, we must recognize the worthlessness of our personal spiritual currency and the inability of our good works to save us.

I never envisioned that the word "poor" would equate to anything good. It was extremely easy for me to see my unworthiness, my emptiness, and my lack of things to offer God. My desperation to be wanted, and my dreaded voids forced me to look for the tangible. The fact that the whole works thing was not an avenue I could take to get to God was music to my ears. I was exhausted in that area. It never ever worked. It was great news to me that I never had to work again to gain God's approval. I became aware that salvation comes first and that works would follow. I experienced this progression to be a wonderful rewarding part of being in the family of God.

This knowledge didn't clear the slate for me or give me the needed tools to protect myself from the world however. My past would follow me in more ways than I ever expected. I would soon find out that I still had voids, and no amount of playing catch-up was going to catch me up. A measure of ignorance still plagued me. I felt at times like a goldfish in an ocean full of water. I couldn't join in conversations at church that involved reminiscing of one's wonderful experiences as a child, or as a college student working on their PhD, or coming from a prominent family who left heirlooms, or missionary families serving in a foreign country to name a few.

This would start a life of always trying to fit in by taking my place that others had chosen for me, not being chosen first, being told what to do, having others form my opinion, often being condemned, and often being shamed. All too familiar to my life of long ago. My decision not to complain or defend myself arose from my ongoing fear that I would have to relive my childhood somehow; some way unbeknownst to me, that would take me back to my childhood life. This would terrify me. This opened up doors for those who saw me as inferior, based on their own position in life, to use it against me, and at times with a smile on their face. I was consistently made aware that I was not as good as others. Not being able to relate on most levels was a constant reminder where I had come from. I spent precious time waiting for someone to simply accept who God created me to be.

I would continue pouring myself into working with children at church and outside of church.

This was a need, so I was afforded a measure of acceptance as long as I kept in my lane. I loved the children and they loved me right back. My time spent with children was very rewarding. As I look back, perhaps I lived a little of my voided life through them. However, it was always rewarding.

Having my own children afforded me a small piece of society that I could finally squeeze into, namely relating to other moms. Although being a mom came easy for me and more importantly, very fulfilling to me, I forgot about me. This was perfectly fine because I found myself protecting, providing, and caring for my children which consistently filled me up. No complaints. I took such pride giving my kids emotionally everything that wasn't given to me.

I felt like the mom of the year. Much of the time there was nothing monetarily in what we did. The outings alone resulted in learning about the world in which one lives; experiences that can last a lifetime in ones' mind. Hiking in the woods, looking at nature. Picking apples in the Autumn. Picking berries in the summer months. Throwing snow balls in the winter. Playing board games of all sorts, reading a ton of books, and crafts for every season. Much laughter and tons of good times, was the norm. Giving them opportunities that I never had a chance experiencing. Swim lessons would be a priority as the result of what I had to go through as a child who couldn't swim. Running and playing, just being kids. Things that were simply not in the cards for me.

Although things were so incredibly different, with so many wonderful times for my kids, no one's life is ever perfect. Parent's decisions can hurt and rock a child's world on different levels. They were not excluded from being affected by a sinful world any more than I was. Their parents' marriage would continue to show that two emotionally unhealthy people do not equate to a successful marriage.

Because I was not prepared emotionally for life itself as a child growing into adulthood, I would feel the sting of my past. I didn't have any choices when it came to a husband either. How was I going to have a clue as to what love is, considering how I had to grow up? Graduating from High School, turning 18 and starting a marriage a week later wouldn't heal me.

When you don't have a chance to heal, a chance to grow, a chance to catch up, and none of the tools needed to do all these things, you don't have much of a chance that your marriage will work either. In saying that, I also believe that God could have healed all wounds. I had no idea who I was in the marriage. I am gaining some knowledge to who I am to some degree, and I give all credit to God. I think that God allows me to re-call these experiences to teach me much.

I will never be whole this side of heaven, but I have all the confidence in the world that I will be complete when I meet my Lord and Savior face-to-face. This knowledge has been so freeing in my life. I feel as though I am reborn. Oh yes, I am twice born; born again by the precious blood of Jesus Christ.

The negative things in my life that plagued me all those years ago seem to be less important now. I attribute this to the marvelous work God began and is doing in my life. I realize that only what I do for Christ will truly last. Keeping my eyes on Jesus alone is absolute key in my healing and growing in him.

Those things that I counted so important in my life as a child and beyond pale in comparison to what is in store for me as a child of Gods' when this life on earth comes to an end.

God equally blesses his own while we are living and breathing on this earth. He has opened so many doors for me since I was a child. I am guilty of taking much for granted. The countless hurts that I endured as a child blinded me at times to what my God was doing in my life. This grieves my soul.

I have experienced his mercy and grace to such a degree that only he and I know to the full extent. The difference in me now is that I fear no one. No one will ever control me, dictate to me on any level, or manipulate me for their own gain. If I allow it; it's on me. Hebrews 13:6 NIV says, "So we can say with confidence, The Lord is my helper, I will not be afraid. What will man do to me"

My God says in Isaiah 54:17 KJV "No weapon formed against me shall prosper, and every tongue which rises against me in judgment, thou shalt condemn. This is the heritage of the servants of the Lord, and their righteousness is of me, saith the Lord". Such comforting words; words that I can now take as my own, words I had no power to own as a child. Indeed, the content of these words was something that I had little power to own as a young adult.

Healing has a new and profound meaning for me as I depend on my Lord and Savior, realizing just how extraordinarily different God's healing is compared to the world's healing. When I reminisce about my life as a child and all that transpired, I now see that it is of the utmost importance that I put my all into Christ alone, and put nothing into the at best fleeting good times this world has to offer.

I am experiencing for myself the true meaning of healing in which God only has the power to bring about. This has forever changed my way of thinking this side of heaven and my dependence on the world. The hopes and dreams that I once had as a child didn't materialize in the way that I had longed for. I defined hopes and dreams for completeness and healing.

God continues to complete me in ways that the world has no power to do. Gods' kind of healing can only come from him. I am overwhelmed because I feel so special and so chosen at times. I know with certainty that what God sees as chosen is polar opposite to what the world sees as chosen. This clinches it for me. No words in any language can describe the peace, his peace, in my heart at this precise moment. I don't want it to end.

Although this feeling will cease to be as intense as it is currently, I will live out this truth from this second forward, knowing with every fiber of my being that my Lord and Savior Jesus Christ personally chose me for his own. Salvation is a one- time act of justification by faith. Sanctification is being done by the power of the Holy Spirit throughout our lives as we live this life on earth in obedience to Jesus Christ.

Seeing my story on paper has awaken me to the reality of just how much I have been controlled by others, to the point of not even knowing who I was. What makes it so much worse is that I allowed much of it in the hopes of having my needs met, those vitally important, life-changing, matter-of-life-and-death emotional needs that God only has the power to meet. The wonderful and life-changing news is that God has forgiven me for putting the world above him. When he looks at me, he sees the righteousness of Jesus Christ. He continues to grow me in his word and will continue as long as I have a beating heart. We will never arrive this side of Heaven no matter how much we gain spiritually while on this earth.

I pray that my testimony will spare another person the hurt, pain, and voids that I experienced, unless of course some of those experiences are needed to bring a person closer to God per his Sovereignty.

We all sin because we are all sinners. The only way out is to be born again into God's family by being reborn. This rebirth begins a new life in Christ Jesus. The old things have passed away, and behold, all things have become new. We are set free from every habitual sin if we yield to the Holy Spirit, who enters our hearts the moment we come to Christ Jesus personally.

What I have the pleasure of looking forward to as a true believer is reigning with Christ for all eternity. Those who were given the world's riches, or gained them on their own without Christ; those who choose to make such riches their source of comfort, their hope, their peace, and ultimately their god will live without the one true God for all eternity. Those who seek after the world's riches, will find it much harder to depend on the true God whom they can't see, than to depend on the gods of this world whom they can touch and see.

I would go on to discover something as devastating, having it all from the world's perspective and having it taken away is even worse. I'm not talking about economic collapse. I'm speaking of when Christ returns, when all that one has gained, enjoyed, and lived for is burned up. The only thing left is standing before God, being told that their destiny has already been determined, resulting in separation from God for all eternity. That which they wanted, they gained, they enjoyed, they lived for, and they ultimately worshipped left no room for a personal relationship with Jesus Christ. They didn't see a need for him which is the lie that the enemy told them, and made them believe.

I heard the importance of storing up for ourselves treasures in Heaven too many times to count as a child. It would begin to take on a whole new meaning for me as an adult. This revelation doesn't diminish the real-life challenges I experienced as a child. Growing in the Lord has allowed me to put some of my childhood deficiencies into perspective.

Being controlled by so many in my little world, I found myself without the permission even to think for myself. Therefore, I missed out not only on many of the tangible things vital to existence, but also on intellectual development. I framed my past with a false narrative so much that I never allowed myself to validate the real hurts, the immense pain and sorrows that were so real in every fiber of my being. This caused me to revisit my past years later and emotionally come to terms with areas in my life that forced me to call my life what it was, instead of staying in denial for the obvious reasons.

If you don't know who you are, and you don't have a clue about the world around you; if you have no positive experiences, no building blocks, and no guidance or direction, how are you supposed to grow and develop in any area?

My circumstances did eventually change, but the hurts and the pain caused by others making me feel less, ostracizing me, and rejecting me remained a tough hill to climb. Now my desperation to fit in was coupled with strings-attached condemnation and manipulation. As an adult, I had the basic needed tools to function in society. I was under the impression that once God had delivered me from poverty, and I had a better place to live, better clothes, and enough money to be independent of the world, all of which afforded me some of the choices that most of society was already accustomed to; I was just like other people, correct? Not a chance. I would find myself reliving many of the same hurts and disappointments when I was a child.

Although I was extremely shy, I was confident that I would mesh right in with other adults at church, well, that didn't exactly happen. I would learn quickly that geographics wasn't enough from others perspective. I still had little in common with other people, and I found it hard to relate to their experiences. I resorted to buying the attention I needed by offering my babysitting skills, cleaning up, and cooking. Resorting back to having no opinion, and accepting that this was my lot in life.

As pitiful as it is to say, the geographics alone was a great improvement for me personally. All relative. My life as a young adult was nearly a 180 degree turn from my life as a child. I personally looked forward in experiencing what my new world had in store for me as an adult. Unfortunately, I would be forced to see those voids that were never filled in my life as a child, would come to surface in my young adult life.

What I would see the secular world engaging in; drinking, smoking, partying, and gambling didn't entertain my thoughts for a second. I see now that my shyness and my voids kept me from that lifestyle. God was always in arm's length from me no matter what situation I was in. He obviously had protected me yet again.

One thing that remained a consistency in my life as a young adult was my place in society. When I encountered someone who had much more monetarily than I had, they were regarded by some to be superior. Their placement in life afforded them a higher degree of esteem than those who were on my social economic level. Those who had a higher education were also elevated above me. Sometimes it was subtle, and other times it was right in my face. I would take any morsel of kindness from such people and accept my position in life. They definitely liked me when I did things to help or when I had something to give. Short of that, I simply didn't belong.

CHAPTER 16

SWEET FELLOWSHIP

1 Thessalonians 5:11

There was something pivotal in my life, something that would slowly change me from the inside out. When I began to work in the inner city as a volunteer cooking for the homeless, I was treated differently. I was the same person who was working endlessly hard to fit in with those in church who spoke for me, placed me and ostracized me.

I spoke the same language. I acted in the same manner. I had the same personality. I was always willing to help were needed. The only difference was how I was treated by these volunteers. I was equal to them. I was most appreciated by the majority. There were some who had more monetarily speaking however it didn't seem to matter, I was accepted and respected. I could relate to them on some levels. No superiority complexes. No exaggerations of themselves. God would use this experience to teach me much.

I came to the realization that the treatment I received as an adult coming out of poverty wasn't personal to me. It wasn't anything that I had done wrong. The people who treated me poorly were human beings who live in a fallen world, and no matter who they thought they were, whom they elevated, whom they favored because of their status, or even who they actually were, no one is more superior than another, based on Gods' perspective. The only perspective needed.

It was my distorted view of how the other half lived. I thought that if I could just have what they had, I would be able to relate to them on some level; somehow gain their approval, and be liked for who I was, and not for what I had to give. This would afford me arrival into society as a whole person. Although I couldn't really comprehend it or wrap my head around it; it was exactly what I had craved as a child.

When I was so warmly accepted and included in the inner city where I joined a team of volunteers with different social economic backgrounds, and different races working together, I would begin to see how people from all different walks of life worked together harmonious in the name of Jesus. Working side by side with those who accept you as you are, allowing you to use your own God given gifts to make up the body of believers. I began to see what emulating Jesus looked and felt like personally. God guiding me to where he wanted to use me, not necessarily where I would have chosen to go.

As a child, I was very sheltered, so much so that it caused me to be invisible and to accept the place in society that others designated for me. Meeting other believers who worked in the inner city who were the hands and feet of Jesus, I began to connect and sense Gods leading. No strings attached was an experience that was not only new to me, but was well received.

As a young adult I realized that I wanted people's acceptance more than I sought God's acceptance. I thought that by working hard, paying, and obeying, I would gain that which would make me whole. Witnessing the good news of Jesus Christ to a spiritually dying world is what God requires us to do as true believers. No ego, no superiority complex, and no competing. This seems to be a good example of being part of the "Great Commission".

I now realize that the only one I must obey is God, and when I do, I get the pleasure of honoring him, praising him, glorifying him, reverencing him, learning about him in his word, and so much more. I consistently thank him that he who has begun a good work in me will not complete it until I meet Jesus face-to-face in the manner in which he chooses, no strings attached, no manipulation and no condemnation. Wow, that's a mouth full.

The improvised life I lived growing up that led to my countless voids made my walk with the Lord here on earth much harder than it had to be. I must take a measure of responsibility for this. I allowed society to control me, instead of allowing God to guide me.

As we read in 1 John 4:18, "There is no fear in love, but perfect love drives out fear, because fear has to do with punishment. The one who fears is not made perfect in love" (NIV).

Those who are in Christ Jesus know the love of God, and this knowledge drives away any fear of condemnation. His love takes away our fear. I simply had to accept and own this truth. I had a choice; listen to the loud noises of the world, or the quiet voice of God in his word.

God's unconditional love which he has showered upon me is evident in my life. I can see more clearly now that I never did fit into my little world as a child, because my little world was controlled by the god of this world, who blinds others to the truth of Gods' word. God adopted me into his family and regenerated me according to his grace, and he has freely given me a new name. What I continue to gain along my journey is sweet fellowship with my Savior.

In John 14:21 NIV Jesus is saying "Whoever has my commands and keeps them is the one who loves me. The one who loves me will be loved by my Father, and I too will love them and show myself to them".

This love is a personal, intimate, relational, affectionate, and committed love from God toward those who belong too, and love Jesus. And yes, that includes me.

CHAPTER 17

TOTAL DEPENDENCE ON GOD

Philippians 4:19

Coming out of the fog that once defined me most of my life allowed me a twofold experience, no more being the pitiful lost girl who had no voice, and no more profound sadness from the many voids that crippled me. And the most profound truth; that God was with me and beside me through it all. God gets all the credit for the desire that he has put inside me to learn about the love of Christ Jesus.

My dependance on my little world absolutely crippled me and robbed me of the God-given peace that surpasses all understanding, and the God-given unspeakable joy. People are people. We are all part of this fallen world; human beings who have sinned against God Almighty. No one deserves God's mercy, his grace or his salvation. By his grace we are saved, not because of anything we might do, have done or will be able to do as long as we have a beating heart this side of Heaven.

Believing that I was always unworthy kept me stuck. I believe that I alone deserved hell for all eternity. I know that if there were a line of people who "deserved" to go to heaven, I wouldn't be in that line. However, I believe that because of who God Almighty is, and because of what he did on the cross of Calvary for all mankind, not just for a few, and not just for the elite, that I am included in the pool of potential candidates per his Sovereignty for spending eternity in Heaven. We are all equal in the eyes of God.

Sin is sin, no matter who commits it, or how small we may claim it to be. We all have sinned and fall short of the glory of God.

I have spent most of my life seeking security, acceptance, and a sense of self-worth from other people. I exercised my free Will without realizing that Gods' way is always best. We all have the choice to use our free Will to grow in our walk with God, or use it for our own fleshly desires. In spite of how I was forced to grow up, in spite of me using my own free Will, my God ultimately kept me alive, when I had no awareness of the dangers around me.

I am disappointed that I had to carry my fears, insecurities, hurts, and pain into my adulthood. When I found myself marginalized as a result of my childhood; this set me back emotionally, equal to what I endured as a child. The life I lived as a child growing up in poverty with nothing to offer allowed others to define me. This kept me crippled in some ways. I must care more about what God thinks of me, sees in me, entrusts to me, and what he does through me, and not on a world that is here today and gone tomorrow.

In spite of being born in poverty, my God was with me, never leaving me or forsaking me. My eyes were on people, not fully on God. I thought my voids defined me based on others' opinions and treatment of me. God needed me to simply keep my focus on him. He needed me to believe that he is enough. I had questioned God as a young child, and at times when I was a young adult. I allowed my circumstances to overshadow his hedge of protection over me.

I was marginalized because I came from a family whom others looked down upon. I wasn't permitted entrée into society because I couldn't relate. I would experience the same rejection that I did as a child because I didn't belong. Not everyone knew where I came from in the beginning. Not relating in all the experiences that others had would take care of that. I would come to accept that no door would be opened for me to walk through, because I couldn't share in those same opportunities that was afforded to others.

Never mind those who had been born with silver spoons in their mouths. Their colleges, careers and successes put them in a class all their own. I would find myself reliving my voided life on a level that I wasn't looking forward to. My idea that helping others could get me the acceptance that I craved, would soon be shot down. The works that I did would bring me nothing but disappointment. I had nothing to offer but my hard work in which others took advantage of without showing me an ounce of true acceptance.

In reminiscing my life, I see clearly that escaping an unfavorable childhood isn't enough to fit into the society you were born into. Now I would be forced to come to terms with the hardcore facts that age doesn't discriminate. I was under the impression that my life as a child was then and there. I had everything in my adulthood that my life as a child didn't afford me. Why did I find myself feeling like the same little invisible girl, who was forced to live a life of poverty?

I would remind myself the fact that my mom was ostracized by those born on the wrong side of the tracks, how could I expect it to be any different for me? Children can pay a very high price for how their moms had to live out their lives. Something no parent wants to pass down to their children.

Being a product of my own environment is a fact that is written in stone in my mind. All these years later realizing just how young my mom was when she went home to be with the Lord Jesus, and how profoundly sad and horrific her life on this earth was, literally hurts my heart on one hand, and immediately causes me to rejoice on the other because she is forever with the Lord.

I still struggle with guilt at times not being able to help my mom more during those years. No tools to help when you are needed most, forces you to relive what you could have done, if you only knew then, what you know now.

Mark 8:36 KJV "For what shall it profit a man, if he shall gain the whole world, and lose his own soul?" This verse would begin to speak to me as I grew in my walk with the Lord. It took a while to resonate, as I reminisced about wanting my desperate needs met tangibly. It would calm my soul years later.

Only those who can relate to their own needs not being met can comprehend this. To watch what others had, as they themselves watch what you don't obviously have is absolutely disheartening. When you see every single adult cross your path that are equipped with the vital tools needed to make it in life, and you are forced to see that it wasn't in the cards for you is yet another setback that you didn't see coming. This causes you to spend your life playing catch up in a world that doesn't notice you.

This can lead to voids that are impossible to fill, causing you to fall further and further behind. Those who are judged, ignored, and ostracized have little hope of getting help. They live devoid lives which costs them dearly. Couple that with ongoing fears of the unknown keeps a person from moving forward.

What God has been teaching me about fear as a result of growing up in poverty is that fear has no hold on me. This I know. What I didn't know is that fear never had a hold on me. I believed a lie from the enemy. My circumstances spoke loud and clear to me. My deficits crippled me. People failed me on many levels. I listened to them all. I worked hard to fit in. I craved acceptance. I desperately wanted others' approval. I set myself up to be used. I was a candidate for anyone's abuse. I was a target for those who had malice in their hearts, the same malice that others had when I was an innocent, ignorant child unprepared for society.

I heard a pastor say that no crisis is greater than Christ. He read Isaiah 41:10 NIV "So do not fear, for I am with you; do not be dismayed, for I am your God. I will strengthen you and help you; I will uphold you with my righteous right hand". To fear is one thing. To be dismayed is quite another. It is important to remain calm in all things, having the assurance of who one is in Christ Jesus. Don't dwell on circumstances that frighten you.

This pastor went on to say; "God can keep us from fear, either by removing the thing we fear, or by subduing our fear of that thing. God has the right kind of presence, the only presence we will ever need. If God can save use from hell, he can be trusted to take care of use while on this earth".

What was missing in me that I never owned these words. I didn't have ears to hear how important it is to allow God, and not mankind to validate you. My circumstances screamed loud and clear that I didn't matter to anyone, which blinded me to Gods' presence in my life. The level of pain and heartache in my life unfortunately took precedence over the truth that God was always right beside me. I focused on what I didn't have instead of what I did have. God was waiting for me to look to him alone.

You find yourself focusing on those whose needs and wants are met. They seemed to set goals. They have many experiences. They could hope and they could dream. They seemed to have victories in their lives. Their lives seemed to be complete and full. I can't blame those who had it all from my perspective. That wouldn't be fair of me to expect others to totally understand. They would have to walk in my shoes to truly relate to what I lived out, and no one is up for that.

I would visit churches that began to preach about having an abundant life while on this earth. I was intrigued. This sounded just like what my peers at school and those kids at my church had experienced. They had everything from the lens I was looking through. However, I would learn that the "abundant life" churches were speaking of was simply false teaching.

God was credited for giving this abundant life to everyone. I would be quickly reminded that my church of long ago never taught this to me. We were taught what the bible says in Colossians 3:2 NIV "Set your minds on things above, not on earthy things".

There are those who think that an "abundant life" on this earth means one gaining material things. The word of God explains it in a different light. An abundant life is eternal. It begins the moment we come to Christ Jesus, accepting him as Lord and Savior over our lives, and it continues throughout eternity. An abundant life is one of spiritual abundance and growth in God's word, drawing close to him, as he draws close to us.

Having a relationship with God causes one to grow in the grace and knowledge of our Lord and Savior Jesus Christ. He makes us Christlike as we walk in obedience to him while on this earth. A true abundant life consists of an abundance of love, joy, peace, and the other fruits of the Spirit. It is eternal life and therefore our interest is in the eternal, not in the temporal.

It is a life far better than anything we could ever imagine this side of heaven. 1 Corinthians 2:9 NIV "What no eye has seen, what no ear has heard, and what no human mind has conceived, the things God has prepared for those who love him". This verse makes me say with confidence, come Lord Jesus come.

As the years would quickly come and go, and the more I depended on God, the more he would reveal to me the truth of his word. I had much to digest, figure out, and make sense of. My hurts were real. My disappointments were real. My fears were real. The rejection I had experienced at the hands of others was real. My unfilled voids were unequivocally real.

Being a product of your environment is not your fault. We are all products of a fallen world. Some of us just fare better than others based on our circumstances whether good or bad. The end result is the same for all of us. Either we accept Jesus Christ as Lord and Savior over our lives, or we don't. The most dreadful problem with the latter is that the only other place to spend eternity is in hell. We have two choices, if we don't choose Heaven, we choose the other by default. There are those who had lots of choices while on this earth, choices not everyone can relate to, and not equal to all. The choice we make between heaven and hell is quite different and equal to all.

I am aware that God uses all our messes to grow us in him. It has been extraordinarily hard for me to wrap my head around all that has transpired in my life from my beginning. I have so many regrets about how I depended on society and seeking answers to the questions that only God can answer.

God knew all about me and permitted me to live an impoverished life. On one hand, I think that I would have been better off had I never met anyone whose life shined a light on the fact that mine was one of deprivation, and on the other hand I am able to see the importance of my growth in society as a result of rubbing elbows with people whose lives are polar opposite to mine.

Unfortunately, neither isolating myself nor mixing with other people protected me from the hurt and pain that God permitted me to go through. God began a work in me upon my conversion as one of Gods' children. A process that takes a lifetime.

My story although similar to others, is personal and unique to me. A person would have to walk in my own shoes to fully comprehend. Only God knows my entire story, and I trust him to help me write it with 100% accuracy, and for those who can't comprehend how I made it, or how I turned out the way I did, my only reply is Jesus Christ, and him alone.

True believers are equally the same Spiritually. We are either truly born again, or we are not truly born again. We have different God given gifts. We have our own unique personalities. We may speak differently based on our backgrounds. We can have unique experiences that others may not have. We may say the same thing in a different way. We can take a different approach in explaining Gods' word, but the end result will always align with scripture.

My prayer is that I might help someone avoid having to jump over some of the hurdles that I had to jump over. I just can't imagine that God would have said no to someone wanting to help me, before I developed those voids that led me down that hopeless road of seemingly no return.

It's a given that wrong choices made by parents can set their children up for failure. This can make life harder for them to achieve their personal goals. Being born in poverty is just one example. Being voided in most areas of life is quite another.

Many people are monetarily poor but not crippled. Many children who don't have a father in the home aren't crippled. Many children who don't have extended family aren't crippled. Many children who have sick moms aren't crippled. Many children growing up in dysfunctional homes can still have the needed tools that prevents them for being crippled. Many children who are ignored and rejected aren't entirely crippled.

Why did my circumstances prevent me from gaining the needed tools that would have prevented me from failing in most areas of my life?

Was insight and discernment somehow not utilized back when I was growing up? Couldn't someone tell how incomplete I was to an absolute fault. Was I an expert at keeping my feelings so deeply hidden, that no one ever noticed? "Expert" is a term that didn't apply to me on any level.

Did someone communicate to me in actions and deeds regularly that I didn't matter. Was I told at such a young age that I am nothing? Too young to remember, however subconsciously owned it. Did the absence of physical touch begin my emotional downfall?

Children whose voids that are left unattended will result in emotional paralysis. Even worse, the voids will follow the person into adulthood as it did for me. This sets one up to relive the same rejections, hurts and heartaches as they did as a child on a much larger scale. The sad part is that there are those who see a wounded person as weak and vulnerable, and they use it for their own personal gain.

A memory of "strings attached" would flood back to my mind as I found myself trying to put my life in perspective as an adult. I have grown along the way on many levels, perhaps merely by way of experiences if nothing else. The hard part is sometimes I let my guard down revealing my wounds that were coupled with the desperation to fit in, and I find myself reliving the pain that so defined me long ago.

I still ponder what came first, my unrealistic desire to be like everyone else based on what life afforded them that I was forced to watch day in and day out, or those crucial needs created by God that were never met by people whom God entrusted me with.

I am confident that if my needs were met as a child, my life experiences as a young adult would have taken on a whole new path for me. A path that I can only imagine. "Normal" comes to mind, whatever that means. One thing is for sure "Normal" had a much different meaning for me.

With all that to say, I know with certainty that God heals, and he restores and opens doors that only he can open. He makes a way when there seems to be no way. He performs miracles, and he makes what society deems impossible, possible. I am a living testament to this. With God all things are possible. He can equally make the seemingly possible by the world's standard, impossible according to his Sovereign Will. He has always been in control, and he will always be in control.

If my story can help someone see that Jesus Christ is all the hope they will ever need, this would help to make how I had to live a little less painful. It would be very rewarding to see that my life as a child growing up in poverty has benefited one person. My experiences may have similarities to the lives of other people, but I have never found anyone who could truly relate to my life in how I had to live it out. Long ago, I wanted that one person to relate to me on some level. Being far removed from my childhood, and looking back, I would find it extremely hard to meet someone who has walked in my shoes. Writing my life experiences down is one thing, meeting someone who had to live a life equal to mine would absolutely break my heart. However, I can see how God could use this experience to bring him glory.

With much rejoicing, I am looking forward to reigning with my Lord and Savior for all eternity. I know based on scripture that he will not return until everyone has had an opportunity to hear of his good news. I know as long as I have a beating heart this side of heaven, God is still growing me in his word and maturing me in my faith.

I am seeing just how temporary this life on earth really is. I am joyfully seeing more clearly what storing up treasure in heaven looks like for me personally. It involves serving the Lord and his people and enduring persecution because of who I am in Christ Jesus. It involves unconditionally loving others and sharing the gospel. It involves obeying God in all things and demonstrating the fruits of the Spirit in my life; a continual process by God.

If I choose the world and its desires, I commit myself to storing up earthly treasures. On the other hand, when Jesus is my true treasure, I devote my life to living for his glory, and winning souls for Jesus Christ, as he works mightily through me.

As a child, I chose the world out of ignorance because my needs were never met. When I saw the needs of others being met and their wants being granted, I felt cheated, unloved, and rejected. One thing led to another. I came to think that not only did I not matter to anyone, but I was worthless. I lived in every way invisible from the inside out.

However, the good news is that I am no longer leaning on the world to guide me, direct me, or teach me. They all failed me and that was the way it was supposed to be. Only God has the ability not to fail us. We will always fail each other. Reading the word of God daily in its rightful context is our only hope in learning how we are to live this life on earth as true worshippers of Jesus Christ, as we trust and obey him in all our actions, words and deeds.

Second Timothy 2:15 NIV "Do your best to present yourself to God as one approved, a worker who does not need to be ashamed and who correctly handles the word of truth".

Exegesis means "to lead out of." What does the passage mean; how does it relate to the rest of the bible; and how should this passage affect my life. Allowing the text to speak for itself is crucial to understanding God's word. Exegesis is concerned with discovering the true meaning of the text, respecting its grammar, syntax, and setting. Exegesis causes us to agree with the Bible.

Eisegesis, on the other hand, means "to lead into" what you want the scripture to say to you. This will often lead to misinterpretation. The interpreter injects his or her own ideas into the text, making it mean whatever he or she wants it to mean. This is a mishandling of the text. Eisegesis is concerned only with making a point, even at the expense of the meanings of words. Eisegesis seeks to force the bible to agree with us.

When I was young and my teachers gave me a bible, they encouraged me to just read it. We weren't given multiple choices in how to us it. The bible will always will be the true spoken word of God. I knew from an early age what Deuteronomy 4:2 NIV says: "Do not add to what I command you and do not subtract from it, but keep the commands of the Lord your God that I give you".

It stands to reason that we must allow the bible to speak to us as the Holy Spirit speaks through us if we are truly born again. To not fully understand a passage, and make it say what one wishes for it to say, is dangerous at best.

I was truly blessed to have the foundational truth of Gods' word presented to me when I was a child. God continues to bless me as I build on that foundation. Many of the bible verses that we were encouraged to memorize are still in my memory bank. Many churches today are not as concerned about the memorization of God's word as they are about making church fun for young people, which has little to nothing to do with learning and obeying God's word. His word is truth, and nothing can change the meaning of the word of God to fit a new way of thinking.

> Jesus Christ the same yesterday, to day, and forever. Hebrews 13:8 KJV

> The grass withers, the flower fades, but the word of our God shall stand forever. Isaiah 40:8 KJV

> Forever, O Lord, thy word is settled in Heaven. Psalm 119:89 KJV

Having the truth of Gods' word poured into me was evident in my life. Not having those vital tools needed to function in society was equally evident in my life.

Many things that one may go through can turn out to be positive at some point, and on some level. Even going through an unexpected trauma can have a silver lining if you will. After much healing, one can pick up the pieces, allowing them to move forward. How do you move forward when you are devoid of those critical pieces? I didn't have the needed pieces to pick up and move forward. I had nothing to build on. My unfortunate hurts were in addition to my deep voids that kept me helpless, and feeling hopeless.

The life that I was forced to live out resulted in me not being prepared for any stage of development, and has left me with scars. The same biblical foundation that I needed to build on to have all of Gods' truth is equal to the same "stage of development" foundation I needed to build on to grow in becoming a productive citizen. Being cheated out of those crucial tools has left me less than a person emotionally speaking. My experiences of long ago remain too painful, and much of it simply makes no sense. Years would go by before I would see God using my impoverished life as a testament to who he is on all levels. The unloving extended family I was born into resulted in its own unnecessary pain. My mom was desperate for her family to accept her at all cost. Although she shared so little with me, our talks years later shed some light on what she had to endure throughout her life that I had no way of knowing.

My mom's life circumstances quickly became what was normal for her. Unbeknownst to her, I related to her definition of "normal". The bullying I endured was my norm. Being left out because society didn't gain me entrance was the norm. The paralyzing fear I lived was the norm, and in a classification all its own. Being used and emotionally abused by those who think they were superior was the norm. Being poor economically was the norm. Living in filth was the norm. All these examples include avenues that allows one to escape, to move forward leaving your past behind. What happened to me?

Falling behind in every stage of development causing voids so deep that it leaves you crippled, giving you little hope of ever fitting into a society that so quickly judges you. You are marginalized in your own little world. Voids so deep that even time doesn't seem to heal.

Working hard to please only last for a time. Taking a back seat is equally short lived. Not having an opinion as to not ruffle feathers doesn't gain you any leverage or acceptance. I would find myself giving it all to God yet again as I did when I was a child. The only difference was my age. I would come to the conclusion that it is easier to just be alone. Jumping through all the hoops never gained me what I desperately needed.

To be desperate to fit in blinded me to what God says in Jeremiah 29:11 "For I know the plans I have for you,' declares the Lord, 'plans to prosper you and not harm you, plans to give you hope and a future" NIV. God has a plan and a purpose for anyone who follows Christ. I was surrounded by countless voices who defined me, dictated to me, and others who placed me where they deemed necessary.

When I looked back, I recall my head spinning. The voices were deafening at times. They became part of my very being, or so it seemed. They definitely drowned out Gods' quiet, gentle and loving voice. Voids that were never filled or addressed at every stage of my development didn't prepare me for what I would have to deal with as an adult.

At some point along my life's journey, I would learn that I am responsible for allowing others to continue to dictate, hurt and define me. People will only do to one, what one gives them permission to do. I'm quite sure that I didn't give anyone permission. However, I didn't defend myself, and unfortunately there are those who get by with bad behavior because you don't defend yourself. Why is it that one has to be put in a position to defend themselves when they are treated poorly? Why should one have to emulate someone else's bad behavior to make their point.

Once I started looking to God in prayer and reading his word, I began slowly with inchworm progress to consistently rely on God alone. No more relying on God just when things were going well. Listening now seemed to have a new meaning for me. With much practice in daily reading and prayer, I would hear him above the noise that came from humans. The more I heard God's small quiet voice as I read his word, the more I wanted to please him. The more that I grew in him, the more forgiveness and love he put in my heart toward those who had hurt me over the course of my life.

Challenges that plague us all can result in throwing in the towel Spiritually. All true believers gain the help of the Holy Spirit as they choose to be guided and directed by him. God uses our challenges to fulfill his purpose for our lives. His purpose for our lives often leads us through the valley. No pain no gain as they say. God was changing me from the inside out. God's plan for me started with Jesus and ends with Jesus.

"You will seek me and find me when you seek me with all your heart." "Jeremiah 29:13" NIV. I used to walk up and down a small area of sidewalk approved by my mom and talk to God. No one else listened to me when I was very young, so I found myself talking to God. Was I seeking God, unbeknownst to me? Was he speaking to me and I didn't have ears to hear? I don't remember expecting God to answer me when I talked to him. When I look back at those times, I can see clearly that I had no more expectations of God seeing or hearing me then I did with those in my own little world. Seeing where I am now spiritually, I can say with confidence that I wasn't alone.

We are to seek the things of God not the things of this world. I thought if my needs were met, then I could easily obey Gods' word. The trouble was that I was putting it into an order that suited me. I thought that I knew best. After all, it was me who lived a dreadful life as a child. I even thought that God had allowed me to think this way since he seemed silent at times.

My deficits, my voids, and my desperate needs screamed loud in my ears preventing me from hearing Gods' small voice. God seemed very distant and because he never answered my desperate childhood prayers for deliverance. I would turn my eyes and hears to the world for help.

I believed in my heart that God loved me. That truth was preached every Sunday and Thursday evening in my church. I just couldn't separate God from my own little world. Because I was made to believe that I was less, I came to own it.

Children who grow up without their vital needs being met at home will believe anything they are told by those on the outside. I praise God that my teachers told me his truth. I couldn't verbalize the meaning of salvation in its rightful meaning. I would hear that God's gift of salvation is of greater value than all the world's riches. Unfortunately, I desired both. God has consistently proven to me that he will provide for my basic needs, and because of his bountiful grace, he has given me even more.

He wants me to depend on him in the way I once depended on my own little world, and he wants me to acknowledge the failures. God uses his children in countless ways. Helping someone or being helped by someone is not the same as depending on a world to a degree in which I did. This mindset blinded me in seeing God at times in my life as a child. This mindset followed me into my adulthood. I plead ignorance as a young child. As an adult, I must take responsibility.

I would come to the realization years later, that chronological aging is not synonymous with emotional awareness. Chronological age is a lousy benchmark for making assumptions about human beings. To judge before you gain the needed facts could turn out to be an insult to one's own intelligence. Life experiences that negatively impact a child's ability to meet developmental milestones is no more the fault of a child, than it is the fault of a baby born with a physical handicap. To be made to feel less is sad. To be ignored by those who feel superior is heartless. To be continually ostracized seems cruel.

I learned all too well in my own little world whether it was at school, in my home, or with those whom I would rub elbows with as a young adult, were all marked by emotional paralysis. I am talking about the silence of my scream for attention, acceptance, acknowledgement, and protection, which no one seemed to notice.

I found myself reading about Elijah and immediately related to him when he felt God was so silent in his life. God proved to Elijah that not only had he *not* been silent, but he protected him in ways that he could have never imagined. God is in control, on his throne, and very real in the lives of his children today as he was in the bible times. Trusting and obeying is key.

I finally came to understand that God had not been silent in my life either. He had been involved in every facet of my life. Because I merely existed in life unprepared for society in every way, I accepted what mankind measured out to me. They invited me into their world on their own terms, and my desperation to be wanted and needed, blinded me to what God would do in my life if I simply let go of the fallen world.

I would grow to see that God loved me unconditionally regardless of my life circumstances. Quite the difference in my own little world that I depended on. I would have to begin to walk in obedience to the light that God had given me, before he would shine additional light on the path, he had set out for me. I needed to have his word daily in my head and in my heart, trusting what he says in his word.

If we fail to develop an insatiable appetite over our life for his word, we will find ourselves distant from God. He will seem silent to us. If we are not in fellowship with him on a daily basis, we leave a crack in our hearts for the enemy to sneak in, and use our flesh against us. Satan is most willing to oblige us when we aren't listening to God with our spiritual ears. Satan is the father of lies. That says it everything!

When I am rooted in God's word, desiring to obey his Will instead of my own and others, I am confident that I can go out and do all the things God calls me to do with excellence because God is in it 100%. When I don't take all thoughts captive in obedience to Christ Jesus, I feel alone, weak, and defeated. This means that I should not rely on human thoughts and plans, or put my trust in mankind. The world's knowledge apart from Christ is meaningless, hopeless, and useless. To be victorious in Christ is to depend on him and him alone. Allowing the Holy Spirit to reshape my thoughts and perceptions would begin a new chapter in my life as a follower of Jesus Christ.

In 2 Corinthians 10:4 NIV Paul says that we are to "use Gods' mighty weapons. They have divine power to demolish strongholds. They are used to knock down the strongholds of human reasoning and to destroy false arguments".

Relying on Gods' divine power and not my own would become real in my life. I had no hope of being victorious on my own merits. The problem for me was that I saw the world being victorious from my perspective. They had a sense of fulfillment because they succeeded in whatever challenge they were up against. My challenges in life always equated to pain. There was never an outlet for me. The little tokens of hope I gained from time to time would always prove to be a false illusion.

As I read my bible, I would see what true victory looked like. 1 Corinthians 15:57 "But thanks be to God! He gives us the victory through our Lord Jesus Christ"

When I was in church as a child, my teachers taught us something different from what most churches teach today. We were taught to go door to door witnessing the good news of Jesus Christ, an experience that is still fresh in my mind. Some listened to the good news; many rejected it. Sometimes when I did this form of witnessing my stomach was in knots.

I remember going to a house that was fenced in. I couldn't tell if anyone was home, so I made the executive decision to open the gate and walk in. The house set further back in the yard than the other houses. It had a wide set of steps that led to a large porch. I walked up the steps, and rang the doorbell. After a couple of minutes of no response. I set my bible track as they were called on the table and proceeded to walk down the steps.

I happened to sneeze, and the next thing I saw was a huge dog running from behind the house. He began with this ferocious bark as he was chasing me. All I remember is how fast I ran. I opened the gate and literally closed it in the nick of time. I felt the breath of that dog behind me. As I was opening the gate, my extra bible tracks flew all over the yard. Needless to say, I didn't retrieve them.

As I look back, I see clearly that God was with all of us when we witnessed door to door. We were taught the importance of "Romans 1:16 ESV For I am not ashamed of the gospel of Jesus Christ, for it is the power of God for salvation to everyone who believes, to the Jew first and also the Greek". I didn't understand much, but I believed.

We gave out bible tracts with the salvation message, direct and to the point. I had the needed enthusiasm to drop off the bible tracts. God was orchestrating my steps long before I was aware. To think how innocence and ignorant I was as a child, I could have easily found myself on a much different path. The firm foundation of the gospel of Jesus Christ that I gained when I was growing up is a blessing that I am still benefiting from. We were taught without apology and without wavering what the true salvation message meant.

I can say unequivocally that my experiences of going to church as a child, even with all the voids that I lived out, pale in comparison to the emptiness and devoid-of-much-truth that is prevalent in many churches today. It seems as though mankind is beginning to take over how people read, interpret, and teach the bible. Some pastors do not even quote or refer to the bible when they give a sermon on Saturday night or Sunday morning. Some churches preach as if God is a cosmic genie or Proverbial Santa Claus. Equally scary is the "social gospel message," which can distort the word of God to say what some want it to say. Wanting our ears to be tickled will cheat us from learning Gods' truth.

I was taught there is only one way to God and that is through his Son Jesus Christ, who died on the cross for all mankind once and for all time, and rose from the grave three days later. I discovered years later that "faith in God" in our society was beginning to have a different meaning than what the bible had to say.

I began to hear that many churches today preach that believing in Jesus, singing for Jesus and simply speaking his name was enough for a person to inherit the kingdom of God. I would learn that many Christians believe that saying a prayer saves you; running down an aisle confessing the name of Jesus saves you; or joining a church saves you. Baptism would follow regardless if one knew its meaning. Speaking that you know Jesus is nothing, if Jesus doesn't know you. John 10:14 NIV "I am the good shepherd, and I know My own and My own know me"

Baptism before true conversion is not salvation or nothing spiritually. Baptism after true conversion is everything spiritually. Some churches teach that baptism is sufficient for salvation. Every time I hear, read or see things that are contrary to the word of

God, I am quickly reminded how blessed I was to hear the truth of Gods' word in those informative years.

Having the truth of Gods' word would allow me to react in my spirit whenever a sermon didn't sound right. The truth of Gods' word being replaced with feel good sermons, water downed messages, and bells and whistles of every kind in many churches today are slowly becoming the norm.

The bells and whistles in church for me as a child came at Christmas time when we put on plays about the birth of Jesus. The bells and whistles at many of the churches today ultimately blind many to the truth of Gods' word.

I would experience those who only want a piece or two of God added to the pleasures of this world. The problem with this mindset, is that we absolutely cannot serve two masters. We must choose one or the other. The wrong master Satan will open the door that leads to hell if we stay on his path. The right Master Jesus Christ will open heaven's doors for all eternity for those who heed his call for their salvation.

Along the way I would experience on a personal level what the word of God means when it says that true believers who stand up for Gods' truth will be persecuted. Those in America haven't experienced persecution on the level as other Countries have; yet. The word of God is clear that we will suffer for our faith in Jesus Christ. "In fact, everyone who wants to live a godly life in Christ Jesus will be persecuted" 2 Timothy 3:12 NIV

Hearing verses taken out of context, and preaching from a human point of view added to the word of God is dangerous at best. Telling someone what they want to hear as opposed to telling them what God wants them to hear will lead them down the wrong road. Some aren't aware that this kind of preaching is devoid of Gods' truth. Replacing God's truth with feel-good messages absolve a potential believer of any and all responsibility for being a true follower of Jesus Christ.

People who agree to adopt to such a message obviously have no interest in honoring Gods' Holiness. There isn't a changed mind, or a repentant heart that leads to salvation. No forsaking and turning away from that which has kept them spiritually blind. Such people have no fear of Gods' wrath to come, which is imminent.

Many churches today don't teach that it is our responsibility to read Gods' word to gain knowledge and understanding for ourselves. The word of God says in "1 John 4:1" to test all spirits to see if they are from God. Those who seek only feel-good sermons attempt to think for God, demanding that he give them what they are essentially paying for. All of these practices have caused some churches to devolve into a social club.

I have grown the most when listening to those who preach the truth of his word with my bible in hand. I thank God for giving me discernment, that prevents me from listening to lies or half-truths. Those who misinterpret the bible are keeping their listeners spiritually blinded. My teachers encouraging me to read my bible would be a blessing for me years later. They each had a personal relationship with Jesus Christ that is still evident today.

Those who teach a social gospel message can misuse and abuse scripture that gives the wrong message to the innocent who only hear what God can do for them while on this earth, if they say a particular prayer or join a church. Many focus primarily on doing works to gain popularity. Feeding the poor, and entertaining them without Gods' truth leaves out the most critical message that we all are spiritually bankrupt in dire need of a Savior who is Jesus Christ.

The bible is clear that we are to take care of orphans and widows. We are to share with those in need. We are equally called to give generously, because God loves a cheerful giver. My teachers of long ago shared with those in need locally, and across the globe. I heard all of God's truth from the very people with whom God had chosen to minister to me. It was neither human-ordained nor sugarcoated one bit. We not only read the bible, we memorized bible verses. We had bible sword drills, a verse was called out, and the first to find it in their bible stood up and read it. The winner was rewarded with gum.

Living a life confused much of the time growing up, along with the not so good, the bad, and the horrid experiences that described my life never served me well. To be blessed to have been taught the truth of Gods' word would serve me well nearly a lifetime later. This truth would come to supersede all else in my life.

I see clearly that God had nothing to do with this confusion that seemed to be part of my DNA. He would use it for my good and his ultimate glory as his word says. God gives his children discernment at precise moments when it is needed most. Charles Spurgeon was known for saying "Discernment is not a matter of simply telling the differences between RIGHT and WRONG; rather it is telling the differences between RIGHT and ALMOST RIGHT."

I was protected from the snares of the enemy because I belonged to God. There were times that I missed out on sweet fellowship with God because I allowed my circumstances to derail me. I own this. Moving forward, and in the same breath looking back allows me to see the bigger picture. It causes me to fall to my knees in humble adoration for who God is in my life.

I would learn the true meaning of profession of faith. In my youth, a profession of faith referred to a person's public declaration of his or her intent to follow Jesus Christ as Lord and Savior over his or her life that would result in baptism after true conversion. I didn't know what conversion meant back then, but I know what it means now and it applies in what I am saying. I was taught to open up the bible and read it. I was given a choice, no pressure. God gives us a choice, no pressure.

I didn't understand much about the bible as a child, but I was made aware of my need for a personal relationship with Jesus. No bells and whistles, and no tickling of my ears. I could have used a little more grace, and a little more mercy at times as I understand it now. However, what I did hear and see lived out was God's truth. The focus was sharing the gospel of Jesus Christ. I know some listened, and some didn't by their own omission, and many like myself took it in and God would use it later in my life. Gods' word with not come back void. I'm a good example of this.

My astronomical needs being met by the "bells and whistles" in many churches of today, would have had a profound effect on me as a child born into poverty that would have equated to a mere band-aide, a coverup to the truth of who Jesus Christ is. The enemy is alive and well and is fully aware of how he is keeping this world spiritually blind to Gods' truth. He doesn't have a chance to keep one blind who desires Gods' truth.

My teachers weren't shy in the least to teach us verses like Jeremiah 17:9 KJV "The heart is deceitful above all things, and desperately wicker: who can know it". The pastors of many churches today could not possibly say this to their congregation because it would result in a reduction of attendance. Meanwhile many are perishing without a clue, because words can confuse unless they are presented with its true meaning and understanding of scripture. A very different definition of "clueless" that applied to me as a child growing up in poverty.

Because words do not always reflect the true condition of the heart, a profession of faith does not always guarantee true salvation. Romans 10:9–10 KJV shows the value of a profession of faith in Christ Jesus alone: "If thou shalt confess with thy mouth the Lord Jesus, and shalt believe in thine heart that God hath raised him from the dead, you shall be saved. For with the heart man believeth unto righteousness, and with the mouth confession is made unto salvation".

At the moment of "true conversion", the Holy Spirit takes up residence once and for all in the heart of a true believer. Without possession of the Holy Spirit, a profession of faith doesn't matter. As I grew in the Lord, I would begin to comprehend little by little what the bible says, and the true meaning of being saved.

Our part in salvation is minimal because salvation is free. Only God has the power to open the spiritual eyes that will set one free for all eternity. Our words have no power to save us any more than our works do. Salvation is by grace alone through the gift of faith, not by any words that we speak unless the heart and the mind are changed.

When churches tell their congregations that Jesus loves, and that he forgives, this is true. However, many churches fail to tell their congregations the whole truth of who God is because many don't want to be told to live holy lives as God is holy. Many don't want to be set apart from the world. Many don't want to give up the allures of this world, so they place Jesus into a slot as they live out their lives independent of God without any awareness that they are on the wrong path; the path that will lead to destruction if they don't repent and turn from their ways.

From the moment of conception, all of mankind already had a sinful nature. Sinful behavior would become one of the defining characteristics of our lives. Even after we are saved and have the seal of the Holy Spirit, our flesh cannot completely stop sinning because being saved doesn't remove our sinful nature.

That is why 1 John 1:8–9 KJV says, "If we say that we have no sin, we deceive ourselves, and the truth is not in us. "If we confess our sins, Jesus is faithful and just to forgive us our sin, and to cleanse us from all unrighteousness". This wonderful truth doesn't give us a license to sin.

Satan, the father of lies is the prince of the air, and he will oblige anyone who is driven by the flesh to rob them of their God-given peace. His job is to prevent true conversions of those who are spiritually blind, or to cause true born-again believers to be ineffective in their walk with Jesus Christ, as a result of living in habitual sin. As true believers grow in their walk with the Lord they will be convicted when they gratify their flesh. No one is exempt from the sin that plagues all of mankind. Without the Holy Spirit guiding and directing true believers no one will be victorious.

This knowledge helped me to see those who were superior to me in a different light. We are all the same, all deserving of hell for all eternity, all sinners saved by grace. This saving grace included me even when I was made to believe that I was a second-class citizen.

It wasn't Gods' fault that I grew up impoverished. It was living in a fallen world with fallen people, and we all suffer the degrading and deadly spiritual, moral, and social consequences of sin.

Hearing countless bible stories like the one in Matthew 15:32 KJV showing Jesus' deep compassion for the poor, and his miracles that he performed while he was walking on this earth, was again evident of his deep love for those who were sick, poor and marginalized by society. Perhaps the bible speaking of loving your neighbor as yourself painted a different picture in my mind that caused me to depend on human beings to the degree in which I did. The verses in the bible that speak of helping those who are desperate apparently framed my way of thinking. I looked to the Christian world to help when my mom didn't have the means. This distorted my thinking, and set me up for much heartache.

My mom didn't have any avenues to get help. Her small family turned a blind eye. They all had an abundance. They entertained their neighbors but ignored our needs. Learning this truth never made sense to me. My mom had no choice but to depend on the government to assist her. She simply had no other recourse.

I believed that God could help us, and he did through the government. I trusted him to not allow my mom to die. He didn't allow her to die when I was young and so unprepared for life. I trusted him to get me out of the place I was forced to call home. He didn't, however, he gave me a place to go to hear Gods' word. This wasn't a fancy church with beautiful stain glass windows. He gave me hope in what matters most when this life on earth ceases. By his grace he gave me his Salvation that secures me a home in

Heaven reigning with him for all eternity. He gave me faith to believe when I couldn't comprehend.

There are various kinds of belief or faith, and not all are linked to Salvation. Faith means more than intellectual belief. It involves trust and commitment when we put our faith and trust in Jesus Christ alone, as our own personal Lord and Savior. God wants more than just words relating to him, he wants more than a church building, he wants hearts devoted to him, and obedience to his word.

Before I became aware of how larger churches were operating, I would choose a big church for my children as they grew for the many opportunities it offered to young people; an alternative to what the world had to offer. I would soon discover that there was more focus on electronics games, and all forms of entertainment that superseded the teaching of Gods' word.

Their stance was that they wanted to reach out to the unchurched, and make them feel loved and wanted. They didn't want to be too preachy for fear they may not come back. The watered-down gospel of Jesus Christ was evident week after week. The truth of Gods' word was superseded by fun and entertainment in the name of Jesus and love.

Thank you, Mrs. Wilson, Jan, Bruce, Gloria, Mr. and Mrs. Martin, and others. I realize that I was truly blessed where it matters most! My regret is that I didn't thank those who were so instrumental in my life. I realized years and years later that I didn't always feel so appreciative for what they gave me as a result of my countless needs, and my many wants that wasn't afforded to me. I had to grow up emotionally and spiritually.

Gods' mercy and his grace are the ultimate attributes of his love. The essence of the bible is to love God, and to love people through the lens of Jesus Christ. I see clearly that my teachers of long ago were obedient to God.

They taught me the importance of abiding daily in Gods' word, which shows not only how we can be sure of our salvation, but in addition, how we may be equipped to serve God per his Sovereignty. How to obtain true success in life as true followers of Jesus Christ would be polar opposite to the world's definition of success that I desperately longed to be a part of.

I have what no amount of money can buy, and what mankind could never give. Those things which meant everything to me when I was on the outside, craving to be on the inside, blinded me to what was most important that will last for all eternity.

True faith in Jesus Christ profoundly changes one's life, and sooner or later will cause a person to produce much fruit for Gods' glory. Ultimately, the fruit displayed in our lives is the test of true salvation, and with it comes Holiness. True converted sinners will grow in their walk trusting God with all things. We will never achieve this while on earth, but with a Holy life lived in service to God Almighty, we are closer to hearing the words "Well done thou good and faithful servant".

In spite of who we think we are, or who we have been told we are, or who we think we are not, or even who we have been led to believe we could never be, God says otherwise. "Then Peter opened his mouth and said of a truth I perceive that God is no respecter of persons'" Acts 10:34 KJV. Another verse that should have consoled my very soul.

I still fear at times, but fear doesn't own me. Fear didn't prevent me from being saved and it didn't cause me to lose my salvation. If one is truly born again, one can never lose his or her Salvation. Living in fear was the result of me living in a government housing project with a sick mom who couldn't meet my needs, and a society that used my deficits against me.

I was a child created by God, born innocent and naïve with the same needs that all children are born with. Children can't raise themselves. If their basic needs aren't met by their parent's they will suffer the consequences. Children need physical touch, and affection as they grow. Love is the primary need and foundation of which all other things can build from. Sunday school teachers can't fill in the missing gaps a few hours each week. Other than the obvious, no one knew exactly how my life as a child was playing out. Embarrassment on where I lived, and being afraid that my mom would be judged by others would be the reason for my silence.

I have beat myself up for living in fear. I heard messages on fear being a sin. That brought on guilt. My circumstances were to blame. My fears weren't the result of me not believing or trusting in God. My fears were based on hardcore facts. If I had believed what some say in that Salvation and fear cannot go hand in hand, I would regress back to where society placed me long ago.

What doesn't go hand in hand is a false sense of security that many churches are teaching to their congregation about the word of God. This form of security is man-made and is keeping many people spiritually blinded, in the name of Jesus no less. It is possible to attend a church regularly, sing in the choir, serve in a ministry, listen often to the word of God, do charity work, give money, and serve the poor, and still be unsaved. Isaiah 29:13 ESV "And the Lord said These people draw near with their mouth and honor me with their lips, while their hearts are far from me, and their fear of me is a commandment taught by men". When people's mouths speak something other than what their hearts believe, their lives will show it sooner or later.

"If anyone will come after me, let him deny himself and take up his cross daily and follow me. For whoever would save his life will lose it, but whoever loses his life for my sake will save it." Luke 9:23–24 KJV These verses speak to me loud and clear as I recall my flesh guiding me (with my permission) to fill my many senseless voids. This is another example of how my Lord and Savior kept a hedge of protection around me even when I was unaware.

I can still recall the sense of guilt that would flow through me, when my flesh wanted what others had. I was taught that we are to be *in* the world…not *of* the world and its philosophy. I didn't understand its meaning to the fullest. All I wanted was to be "normal". I could repeat these words, only to discover over and over again that the world had things that I legitimately needed, and wanted. The world had people with whom I wanted to emulate. The world offered experiences that seemed to be safe and morally good. What was wrong with having both. I thought my desire was aligning with Gods' Will. Did I really want Gods' Will to align with mine?

One day I found myself reading the Lord's Prayer with my heart. I had heard it countless times before. I believed it, and I prayed it. I even wrote it on canvas, and hung it on my wall. Reading "Thy will be done" began to take on a different meaning for me as God was growing me in his word. I can see clearly that my walk with

Jesus was becoming stronger and more meaningful in my life. I wanted to really obey my Lord and my Savior in all things. I never expected this part of the Lord's Prayer to touch my heart and convict me as it did.

I realized that to pray "Thy will be done" has a more profound meaning that I either had overlooked, or perhaps I didn't have the ability to fully comprehend its meaning as a child. It is saying that I not only trust God, but I put my full faith in him to do whatever he needs to do to make me more like his Son Jesus Christ. I needed to acknowledge God's right to rule over my life. He was asking that my Will be conformed to his Will, not his Will be aligned with mine. Another example of how God speaks to his children individually and intimately.

"Thy will be done" acknowledges that God has more knowledge than we do, and that we trust his way is best. The more we know God, the more readily our prayers will align with his Will; and then we will truly mean it when we say, "Thy Will be done." Something that took me a long time to say, to actually mean, and at times to really want.

We can then approach God with boldness and also with the confidence that if we ask anything according to his Will, he hears us. Although I understand what "Thy Will be done" is saying to me now, I had no concept when I was a growing up. I just wanted God to fill my extremely deep voids. I wanted him to deliver me from my circumstances. I thought that I knew what was missing in my life that could fill my voids. So desperate to gain anything that would take away my pain, heal my hurts, catch me up in society, and help me to fit in. I had enough of feeling unwanted, inferior, and marginalized by the world I lived in.

My deep-seated legitimate needs superseded and continued to blind me until I began to trust God with all of me. People and things are a mere Band-Aid when applied to human voids and hurts. Only God has the power to truly heal us, and make us whole.

I now believe when I pray, "Thy will be done" to God Almighty, it is the best thing that I can ask for. It is a sure thing. It will not paralyze me. It will not disappoint me, or keep me stuck, or hoping against all hope that someone will come along and rescue me. Only God could totally deliver me. He is the only true and living God of the universe. Indeed, he did rescue me, indeed, he did deliver me.

Our continual obedience in our prayers help to align our hearts with God's heart, until God's Will becomes our highest priority. He promises to listen to us, and to grant us the desires of our heart according to his perfect Will. God is our heavenly Father, and we must allow him to fulfill his purpose in our individual lives while on this earth.

It was very difficult for me from my limited human perspective to tell the difference between the "desires of my heart" and the "desires of my mind." We sometimes find ourselves in a painful process of learning, and we are not necessarily the best judges of what our hearts desire is, or the best predictors of how it will look when we actually receive that which we desire.

The Holy Spirit is our protector and our guide if we would simply trust him and obey him in all things. Even when we can't see what God is doing in our lives, we know as his children that he has not left us to figure it out on our own. No one told me this either. I lived my life trying to figure it out on my own. My unawareness of the world in large caused me to worry about things I didn't know, instead of obeying the things I did in fact know.

Going through the informative years on my own kept me in a fog. No one preparing me, or having anyone to encourage me on a regular basis kept me paralyzed. What my heart and my mind wanted was equal from my perspective. Devoid of critical tools in ones' life is not going to gain you what you need to be successful in any stage of development. Consistently falling behind guarantees that you will stay behind. Living in a fallen world with fallen people who see you as inferior and worthless guarantees your demise in everything you put your hope in.

CHAPTER 18

MY ENDLESS CRY

Psalm 102:1

Have you ever cried yourself to sleep night after night hoping it was just a dream that you would awake from? Have you felt so numb that you can't feel? Have you hurt so bad inside that you feel you may die? Did you grow up so devoid of the crucial tools that are vital to life? Have you ever found yourself screaming inside, but nothing comes out? Ignoring the emotional welfare of a child who doesn't have the building blocks required to move forward in their life leaving them crippled, is abuse.

Have you ever been refused permission to let go, and speak out to defend? If you have, you know that getting really mad and then exploding solves nothing. Frustration builds up inside you to the point that you can't catch your breath. Your cry for help is endless. That was how it was for me. No one ever seemed to notice. I have to believe that they simply didn't notice; to know for certain that I was purposely ignored when I screamed in desperation, would kill me emotionally. Did I hide my pain so extremely well that no one knew?

Were my expectations unrealistic? Did I have the right to need help, to feel love, to be understood, or to get help from those who knew me? To believe that those in my life knew of my desperation, but simply chose not to help has the potential to erase all the years of healing up to this point.

To think that I could relive my life as a child devoid of all tools necessary to move forward in life, I absolutely couldn't. I don't have it within me. I can't go back and relive. I absolutely can't. Then I think, I couldn't do it, God could. I can't do it, God can.

They say what doesn't kill you makes you stronger. I say what doesn't kill you is only restored and made truly alive through Jesus Christ God Almighty, and no one else. Without him I would simply cease to exist emotionally.

I would imagine being a robot controlled by God. If such were the case, then my lack of tools would not have caused me to continue to fail in all areas of life, emotionally, psychologically, mentally, and physically, leaving me with those all too familiar voids that left me hopeless and helpless as a human being.

What went wrong. What was needed to make it right? Where was that one person whom I needed? Why didn't someone notice? Was I paying my ancestors consequences? Why did it take the pervasive extraordinary hurt, the ongoing crippling pain, and the seemingly never-ending disappointments to get me where I am today with my Lord and Savior?

What do all of these circumstances, hurts, and pains say about me? Am I less than the average human being whom God created? Had I fallen between the cracks? Did I give "invisible" a new meaning? Was I the one responsible for the fact that I grew up ignorant, unprepared, and incredibly voided? What is the answer?

Why do I have to be constantly reminded of how I had to grow up by those who feel superior? Escaping from my childhood, and providing for myself as an adult turned out to be in many ways a lateral move. I wanted complete wholeness. God gives complete wholeness upon salvation. Why couldn't I have complete wholeness in areas of my life that permits one to be productive? On some levels, it is a matter of life and death. Is that too much to ask?

What I needed as a child is what I need as an adult: unconditional love, acceptance, and help and guidance in those areas that I wasn't prepared, or equipped for. I needed understanding in the areas of my life with those I couldn't compete with. How does one wrap their head around such hurt and pain caused by others who are made to believe by society that they are better?

How does one overcome such formidable challenges, when one is unequivocally unprepared and ill-equipped, that encapsulates ones entire being? How can a person so voided truly help someone else? How do you make a positive dent into society, when you have absolutely nothing to offer? How does someone find themselves in a society that is constantly sizing you up, speaking for you, and through you?

I was forced to relive my past at a time when I was under the impression that I was finally "normal," only to be told by others, by way of actions, and in deeds that I didn't fit. How am I supposed to feel "normal" if I can't fit in anywhere? Instead of being chosen by others, I am ostracized, disrespected, and ignored.

It wasn't material things that I necessary lacked. I had what I needed to be independent of the world. There will always be those who have less, and those who have more. I was so far from where I was as a child monetarily, that it didn't matter that there were those who had far more than I did. Such things didn't have the same hold on me as they did when I was growing up. What I lacked was the needed acceptance from others, unconditional love, and respect for who I was. I lacked appreciation from others who God made me to be. I wanted society to accept me so that those voids of long ago would be filled up, or at least prevent the hole from going deeper.

This had nothing to do with the void in each of us that only God can fill. This had nothing to do with depending on the world to complete me as I did when I was a child. This had nothing to do with having my own way. This had nothing to do with attempting to emulate others of their material possessions. This had nothing to do with wanting to be in their made-up bubble.

Christians are encouraged to have personal contact with other believers so that we can encourage one another to live out the faith we proclaim. We are called to "hold fast" through our own spiritual maturity. Growing in faith together means that there are others whom we can call on, depend on, and encourage as we walk this walk for Jesus Christ. "Do not merely look out for your own personal interests, but also for the interests of others". Philippians 2:4 NASB

I will never be able to wrap my head around my growing-up years, except to say, that God knows all things and can change things on a dime according to his Sovereign Will. My story is not fully written as long as I have a beating heart, so therefore I must trust God alone to finish my story.

Children can and do pay their parents' consequences, but it doesn't mean that once we become adults, we are useless or ill-equipped to carry out God's plan for our lives. It's not by human efforts that we even serve God. It is by his abundant grace and his bountiful mercy which brings us to him in fellowship, if we put him first in our lives. He gets all credit and glory for who he is, and what he does through his true born-again believers. What I hear society screaming is one thing, and what I hear God saying as owner and author of the universe is quite another.

God can still use each of us to accomplish his purpose. We are all broken vessels in need of constant repair. We discover our true identity in Christ Jesus the closer we draw to him. The promise of realizing our identity in Christ causes us not to lose sight of who we are destined to be. Allowing my emotions to rule me has caused me great distress and has cost me sweet fellowship with my Lord and Savior for far too many years. Because my circumstances screamed loud and clear I was alone, I believed that I was all alone. My choices were slim to none. Fear of the unknown sets in and you just survive.

The Bible's definition of *trust* is not synonymous with fighting fear on our own, giving in to constant worry, depending on others, or attempting to figure things out on our own. Trusting is what a believer does because of the faith we have been given. Its believing in the promises of God no matter what circumstances we may find ourselves facing. I heard and read this long after I grew up. I needed to hear this throughout my life, on a level that I could comprehend. I needed to be told that even those whose lives appeared perfect go through trials and heartache they wouldn't choose. Lack of knowledge hurt me to the core. Finding yourself all grown up should be the excitement of a new chapter in your life. This brings on a strong feeling of eagerness to what lies ahead for you. If you arrive in adulthood crippled, you can't share the same enthusiasm of those who lived a different life than you did. If my life remains the same as it was when I was a child, my actions and reactions will remain the same. I would allow society to continue to define me resulting in me listening to the wrong voices that kept me crippled, instead of allowing God to define me, that would have sustained me.

I have felt much guilt on one hand, and conviction on the other, for much of my life. I put my trust and my energy into those who constantly showed me how unworthy I was, because I was born on the wrong side of the tracks. I spent my life trying to convince others that I had something to offer, and was willing to be last just to have a spot in their society.

When I gave myself permission to look back, I began to see clearly that I put everyone above God without even realizing it. When you are failed by the society in which you were created to be in; your life will tell a much different story. It doesn't excuse my reliance on mankind, it explains the how's and the why's of my life.

I would learn the definition of both true guilt and false guilt, as I matured in my walk with the Lord. The definition of conviction and the definition of guilt comes from two opposite sources. Conviction will restore, while false guilt will destroy.

As I began to write my story, with every single word, my life as a child would flash right back in my mind. Ignoring my past so that I could move on while anticipating a better life ahead, was stopped in its tracks for what lied ahead for me in the adult world. I would discover it had less to do with needed funds and everything to do with pain.

A life full of voids that resulted in crippling pain dictated my life on every level. Living in a society that has its own set of rules, with its own criteria, and its own prejudices doesn't afford those who can't relate to start over in life. It sets you back to such a degree that the hope of fitting into the adult world is shot down before you find yourself standing on your own two feet. It can even take away the last bit of hope that you thought you gained in transitioning from a child to an adult.

When a heart is broken again and again, the wound never seems to have a chance to heal. Awakening a wound brings back the familiar story of how the pain originally began.

God chose me before the foundation of the world as his own, and I belong to him and him alone. This knowledge would begin to supersede all that I went through as a child growing up in poverty. It would become personal to me as God continued to grow me per his Sovereignty.

"But you are a CHOSEN RACE, A royal PRIESTHOOD, A HOLY NATION, A PEOPLE FOR God's OWN POSSESSION, so that you may proclaim the excellencies of him who has called you out of darkness into His marvelous light." I Peter 2:9 "NASB"

I will conclude with a prayer:

Dear God,

Thank you for not only hearing my prayers, but answering them in your own perfect timing according to your Will for my life. Thank you for your bountiful mercy and your abundant grace that you have lavished on me because I belong to you. Thank you for choosing me and calling me your very own.

Thank you for my faith in you. Thank you for your unconditional love for me, which lifts me up in such a way that keeps my eyes focused on you, and makes my spirit soar like an eagle. I pray that you will use this book to bring others to you in faith. I pray that it will help encourage those who can relate to my life experiences.

I pray that I may never turn a blind eye or deaf ear to anyone who is plagued by a life that was as voided as mine. I pray that my story will impact someone who was left to figure things out on their own because no one seemed to notice.

I am aware that my flesh wages war against my spirit, and I pray that I will keep my thoughts on you when my fallen flesh tries to derail me, causing my eyes to look away from you. I confess that I can do nothing on my own Lord Jesus. Help me to learn a new meaning of humbleness.

I thank you God for the hope that I have in Jesus Christ alone. Thank you that I not only profess Jesus Christ as my Lord and Savior with my mouth, but I was immediately indwelled with the Holy Spirit the moment I became truly born again. Help me to be completely yielded to the Holy Spirit so that he can have freedom to occupy every part of my life as he guides and directs me according to his Will.

Give me the courage to walk in the newness of life and be ready to give an answer for the hope that I have in you.

Teach me to offer up to you a heart of gratitude every day for all that you do for me, and through me. Help me be a vessel for you so that I may serve you mightily in all my actions, words, and deeds. Use me for your Great Commission. I plead with you to give me the courage I need to give thanks in all my circumstances, knowing that you Almighty God can bring good things out of even difficult situations.

Give me the strength to follow you in tough times as well as good times. Give me the needed confidence that you are in control and will work all things out for my good and for your ultimate glory.

Help me to leave my anxiousness at the cross, knowing with confidence that you will direct my path as I listen to your quiet voice. Give me discernment so that I will be able to flee from the enemy's lies and tactics.

I love you Jesus for the ironclad fact that you loved me first because you are the definition of LOVE 1 John 4:10 KJV "Herein is love, not that we loved God, but that he loved us, and sent his Son to be the propitiation for our sins"

Thank you for my Salvation "Acts 4:12" NIV Thank you for my Regeneration "Titus 3:5" NIV Thank you for my Justification "Romans 5:9" NIV Thank you for my Sanctification "Acts 20:32" NIV Thank you for my Glorification "Romans 8:30" NIV

In the precious name of Jesus Christ,

Amen and Amen

FORGIVE ME LORD

For depending on this fallen world...
Forgetting the power of your sword...
For doubting when things never looked good...
For attempting to depend on man thinking I could...
For choosing to do things all on my own...
For having to remind me I am no one's clone...
For the many unnecessary tears that flowed down my face...
For self-condemnation that left me feeling disgraced...
For allowing others to define who I was meant to be...
For accepting society's opinion that was best for me...
Until that moment I gave it to my Creator...
My God choosing me I would own years later...
Knowing who I am in Christ Jesus alone...
Forever this side of Heaven a lesson in me sown...
Growing in my Savior is my greatest story...
Given by God who gets the credit and all the glory...

Printed in the United States
by Baker & Taylor Publisher Services